シリーズ 記録遺産学論考

市民のエンパワーメント

21世紀における
博物館・図書館の機能と社会的使命

Wang Li 王 莉

Empowerment of Citizens

Social Mission and Functions of Museums and Libraries in the 21st Century

樹村房

まえがき

　コンピュータの出現によって図書館の書誌情報検索が変容したように，インターネットの出現によって博物館の姿も変わりつつある。すでに社会的インフラとなっているインターネットや SNS によって，博物館の情報提供の方法も，また当然のことながら運営方法も変化している。

　博物館は図書館の情報と結びつくことによって，あるいはデジタル化されたアーカイブズによって，これまで成し得なかったことが，ますます可能となっていくであろう。今後，博物館や図書館がどのように進化していくのか興味深いテーマである。

　本書は筆者がこれまで発表してきた論文をまとめたものであるが，原著は英文である。それを日本語に翻訳して本書の前半とした。本来ならば，論文ごとに英文－邦訳とすべきところだが，論旨の流れや書籍としての形式を整えるために，邦訳－英語原著論文というやや変則的な構成にしていることをお断りしておきたい。

　浅学の身であることは認めざるを得ないが，博物館での実務経験のあと，一大決心をして研究の道に足を踏み入れてから 10 年が経過した。この 10 年をひと区切りとして，これまでの研究成果をまとめておきたいと思い，幸いアメリカのある財団から出版助成を得たため，こうして出版することが可能となった。

　これまで研究を指導してくださった筑波大学大学院の指導教授をはじめ，励ましてくださった多くの人々に感謝したい。目に見えない研究成果を本という形に可視化してくださった樹村房の安田愛さん，出版を引き受けてくださった大塚栄一社長に感謝申し上げる次第である。

目次

まえがき　1

序　章　危機に立つ国家：生涯学習に向けたアメリカの物語 ──── 8

第1章　地域遺産に立脚した良知主導型文化の構築：21世紀における博物館の社会的使命 ──── 18

第2章　博物館建設における課題と好機：日中の比較による歴史的・社会的見地から ──── 22
　2.1　背景：日中の奇跡的な経済発展　23
　2.2　博物館の社会的使命　25
　2.3　博物館，イノベーション，そして持続可能な社会発展　26
　2.4　日本と中国から学ぶこと　28
　2.5　結語　31

第3章　ミュージアム2.0：ソーシャルメディアによるサイバー空間での拡張展示 ──── 35

第4章　栄光と夢：サイバー空間時代における博物館の社会的使命の再考 ──── 42
　4.1　博物館近代化への道　42
　4.2　メガトレンド　43
　4.3　新しい潮流　45
　4.4　結語　46

第5章　博物館，図書館，アーカイブズを変容させる触媒としてのデジタルエンゲージメント：フィールド自然史博物館の事例研究 ———————————— 49

 5.1　背景　49
 5.2　MLAにとっての課題と好機　50
 5.3　フィールド自然史博物館を研究対象とした理由　51
 5.4　デジタルエンゲージメントの活用　53
 5.5　MLAの社会的使命　57
 5.6　博物館の戦略的位置づけの認識　57
 5.7　ソーシャルメディアは水路か洪水か　60
 5.8　教訓　62

第6章　情報科学による市民のエンパワーメント：サイバー空間における博物館，図書館，アーカイブズ ———————————— 66

 6.1　セカンド・エコノミーと社会発展　66
 6.2　博物館の社会的使命と公共サービスの再考　68
 6.3　サイバー空間における課題　69
 6.4　MLAの戦略的管理　71
 6.5　MLAと21世紀型スキル：アメリカにおける博物館・図書館サービス機構（IMLS）の構想　73
 6.6　教訓　75

あとがき：情報を知性へと変換すること，知性を英知へと変換すること
79

Table of Contents

Introduction
    A Nation At Risk — An American Tale for Lifelong Learning ——— 82

Chapter 1
    Building Conscience-Driven Culture Based on Regional Heritage: Social Mission of Museums for the 21st Century ——— 91

Chapter 2
    Challenges & Opportunities in Museum Development: A Historic-Sociological Perspective — China versus Japan ——— 95
    2.1 Background: Economic Development Miracles in Japan and China   96
    2.2 Social Mission of Museums   98
    2.3 Museums, Innovation and Sustainable Social Development   99
    2.4 Lessons We May Learn from Japan and China   100
    2.5 Conclusion   103

Chapter 3
    Museum 2.0: An Extended Exhibition in Cyberspace by Social Media ——— 109

Chapter 4
    The Glory and the Dream: Rethinking the Social Mission of Museums in the Era of Cyber Space ——— 115
    4.1 Museum Modernization in Japan   115
    4.2 Mega Trends   116
    4.3 New Trends in museum sector   118
    4.4 Conclusion   119

Chapter 5
> Digital Engagement as a Catalyst in Transforming Museums, Libraries and Archives: A Case Study of the Field Museum of Natural History ——————————————————————— 121
> 5.1 Background   121
> 5.2 Challenges and Opportunities for MLA   122
> 5.3 Why The Field Museum   122
> 5.4 Digital Engagement   125
> 5.5 Social Mission of MLA   129
> 5.6 Awareness of Strategic Positioning of Museums   129
> 5.7 Social Media, Waterway or Flood   132
> 5.8 Lessons Learned   134

Chapter 6
> Empowerment of Citizens with Informatics: Museums, Libraries and Archives in Cyberspace ——————————————————— 138
> 6.1 2nd economy and social development   138
> 6.2 Rethinking the social mission and public services of museums   140
> 6.3 Challenges in cyberspace   141
> 6.4 MLA strategic management   142
> 6.5 MLA and 21st century skills: IMLS initiative in the U.S.A   144
> 6.6 Lessons learned   146

Epilogue
> Turning Information into Intelligence Turing Intelligence into Wisdom   150

*** ***

索引   153
Index   154

市民のエンパワーメント
21世紀における博物館・図書館の機能と社会的使命

序章

危機に立つ国家
生涯学習に向けたアメリカの物語

　かつて情報科学による市民のエンパワーメントに関する研究を進めていた時に，アメリカの教育政策に関する膨大な情報に触れる機会があり，当時アメリカ議会が公表した教育に関する1983年の白書「危機に立つ国家」を読んで筆者は大きな衝撃を受けた。この報告書は，ドナルド・レーガン大統領下で設置された「教育の卓越性に関する国家委員会（The National Commission of Excellence in Education）」がまとめたものである。当時，アメリカはソビエト連邦と並んで世界の超大国のひとつであった。それなのになぜ，アメリカは「危機に立つ国家」だったのであろうか。どこから戦争行為が生まれるというのであろうか。

　　非友好的な外国の政権が，現行の平凡な教育をアメリカに課そうと試みたとしたら，我々はそれを戦争行為と見なしただろう。現状では，我々は自らこの事態を招いている。我々は，スプートニク・ショックを受けた学生たちの業績の恩恵まで浪費してしまったのだ[1]。

　この報告書は，アメリカの繁栄，安全保障，礼儀正しさは，凡庸な教育という潮流によって侵食されており，確固たる卓越性を誇っていたアメリカの商業，産業，科学，技術革新，世界中の競争相手に追い抜かれてしまったという事実を明らかにした。そして，知識，学習，情報，特殊技能を伴う知性が，かつて世界に貢献した奇跡の医薬品や合成肥料，ブルージーンズなどに代わる，国際商取引の新たな原材料になるだろうと予想していたのである。

序章　危機に立つ国家

　歴史的出来事は，常に驚くほど一致している。ディケンズの小説『二都物語』では，第二次産業革命前夜の様子が次のように描かれている。

　　あれは最良の時代であり，最悪の時代であった。叡智の時代にして，大愚の時代だった。新たな信頼の時代であり，不信の時代でもあった。光の季節であり，闇の季節だった。希望の春であり，絶望の冬だった。人々のまえにはすべてがあり，同時に何もなかった……[2]。

　第三次産業革命前夜，アメリカの先見的指導者たちは，職場において加速し続ける競争の世界，危険が増大するばかりの世界，そしてさらに機会が拡大している世界に対応するためには，「学習社会」が必要であると注意を喚起した。この学習社会とは，あらゆる人に生涯学習に向けて全能力を発揮する機会を提供するという価値観，およびそれに基づく教育制度へのコミットメントを意味する。

　学習社会とは，小・中・高等学校や大学などの伝統的な機関のみならず，図書館，美術館，博物館，科学センターなどで構成されている。教育の目標は，個人のキャリア目標を達成し，人生の価値を高めることである。特に，多元主義と個人の自由を誇る国では，自由で民主的な社会と共通文化の育成に向けて，高いレベルの教育を共有することが不可欠である。

　若い時に公的な教育機関で学習することは，一生を通して学ぶための不可欠な基礎を成す。情報化時代にあって，個人のスキルは瞬く間に時代遅れとなると考えられるため，今後，生活の質を高いレベルで維持するためには生涯学習が必要となる。アメリカ人は，最高の産業システムや最強の軍事力を開発するよりも教育を重視したのである。彼らは教育をこの両方の基礎を成すものと理解していた。

　報告書は，州および地方の高校の卒業要件を強化し，最低限，英語，数学，科学，社会科，コンピュータサイエンスという新たな基礎5教科を全生徒が学ぶべきであると勧告した。大学への入学を目指す場合，高校で2年間外国語を学ぶことが，それまでの履修分に加えて強く推奨されている。

アメリカ人は，教育が社会の物質的な幸福の原動力のひとつであることを理解している。教育は現代社会の共通の絆であり，私たちを世界中の他の文化と結びつけてくれる。彼らは，自国の安全が，今日もこれからも，教育を受けて自信に溢れた人々の知力，技能，そして精神に主に依存していることを知っているのである。

　偶然にも，筆者はこの報告書を自分自身のガイドラインとして用い，生涯学習に取り組む必要性，博物館や図書館を市民の発展のための拡張空間として活用する方法，そして博物館や図書館の社会的使命と公共サービスによって社会発展を達成するためには何をなすべきか，を学んだのである。

時間，空間，そして自分自身を越えて：筆者の研究の探究の道

　本書は 2009 年以降に発表した論文を集めたものである。博物館，図書館，アーカイブズの役割と社会的使命に対する博物館教育者の視点を通した，生涯学習に関する研究の歩みの記録である。これらの論文には，社会学の応用によって行ったアメリカ，イギリス，日本，および中国の博物館および図書館のケーススタディによる比較研究が反映されている。

　筆者は比較的名前の知られている中国の歴史博物館で国際交流のための学習と開発を担当していた。大学卒業から 6 年間のキャリアの中で，筆者は世界各国から訪れる数百人の政治，宗教，事業者団体，国際交流機関のリーダーたちと顔馴染みになったが，彼らからは常に知的な質問を投げかけられた。多くの来館者からの質問によって，筆者は 2008 年の世界的な金融危機の根本的原因を探るために，歴史を鏡として使う方法を考えるようになった。ミレニアム世代の大半と同じように，当時，筆者はコミュニティ開発の問題にそれほど注意を払っていなかった。アメリカの銀行家の著書『良知の言葉』(*Language of Conscience*) を読んだことが契機となって，筆者は，季節雇用の博物館研究員という身分を離れ，筑波大学大学院図書館情報メディア研究科の博士課程で学ぶことにした。

　本書の各論文は，博物館・図書館の使命と公共サービスの役割を考察するための特定の見地を提供する自己完結型の資料となるように構成されており，情

報科学による市民のエンパワーメントを究極の目標としている。以下，要約を兼ねて本書の構成を記しておく。

地域遺産に立脚した良知主導型文化の構築：21世紀における博物館の社会的使命【社会的使命という観点】

　第1章は，国際博物館会議アジア太平洋地域連盟（ICOM ASPAC）日本会議2009で発表した筆者の最初の論文である。2008年に生じた金融市場の失敗が社会に与えた影響を理解しようと試みていたとき，良知に基づく基本的価値観の欠如が主な原因のひとつであったことを学んだ。

　一般的にいえば，博物館の主たる機能は，調査，収集，保管，展示，教育などと考えられている。今日の世界では博物館を観光名所として見るため，地域遺産の保全と促進をどのように認識すればよいのかという第1の課題に直面している。第2の課題は，博物館専門家に対する課題である。地域遺産の活用によって良心主義文化を構築するためには，どのように体系的なアプローチを組み立てていけば良いのだろうか。

　博物館を知識仲介の家として見るには，知識仲介のライフサイクル全体をはじめから終わりまでカバーできる完全なプロセス開発を導入する必要がある。このプロセスは，知識の創造，知識の獲得，理解と吸収，活用，そして知識の普及，という段階に分類することができる。

　インターネットと情報技術は，従来の学習方法を変えただけでなく，私たちの基本的価値観にも影響を与えた。今日，私たちの価値観は，エンターテインメント性と利便性を重視する，商業化されたメディアや情報源によって形づくられている。コア・バリュー（中核的価値）の創造に加えて，経済発展のために最新の技術を適用する方法を模索することは，今日の世界文明の重要な使命となっている。

　文化は本質的に無形であるため，その振興は容易ではないが，博物館のネットワークが，過去，現在，未来を繋ぐだけでなく，良知を通じて自国と他国を繋ぐ目に見える方法となり得るであろう。博物館と図書館は現代社会における文化的アイデンティティの表現であるからだ。

21世紀における博物館の歴史的社会的使命としての，地域遺産に立脚した良知主導型文化の構築は，筆者にとって最初の探究テーマとなった。

博物館建設における課題と好機：日中の比較による歴史的・社会的見地から【社会学的・経済的観点】

第2章は，クロアチアのザグレブで開催された国際博物館会議・教育と文化活動委員会（International Council of Museums: International Committee for Education and Cultural Action, 以下 ICOM CECA と略）2011 で発表した論文である。博物館が社会の中で果たす役割を理解するため，日中の比較研究を通して社会発展と博物館の発展を関連づける研究を行った。

2010 年現在，中国は 30 年にわたる自由貿易政策により，日本を追い越して世界第 2 位の経済大国となっている。同時に，中国における博物館の数は，1978 年の 300 館から 2010 年には 3,000 館に増加した。一方，日本では 1945 年の 145 館から 2003 年には 5,000 館へと増加した。

日中のさまざまな経済発展段階において博物館が担った公共サービスの役割を歴史比較方法論に基づいて研究することで，地域経済の成長を通した文化の発展の影響に関する新たな展望が明らかになるものと期待できる。歴史社会学的方法論を適用することで，日本と中国における，経済発展と対比させた博物館建設の歴史を，時代と地域別に調査した。この歴史比較研究のため，質的・量的手法を組み合わせることとした。この研究の目的は，時代，国民，地域社会，および社会・経済発展などの要素を用いて，教育とイノベーションにおける博物館の役割を理解することであった。

比較を容易にするために 5 段階のアプローチを設け，日本が他の先進国と同様の問題に対処するにあたり，いかに博物館を利用して社会教育制度を発展させたかを明らかにするとともに，中国が高度経済成長にともなっていかに博物館制度を発展させてきたかを把握したい。

日中を比較する際の主な特徴点は，「政府主導　対　学術団体主導」「公教育を通じた経済成長　対　大衆政治運動」「ランドマークの開発を通した成熟　対　文化遺産の保護」「博物館の病変から生じる神話　対　ハードウェアの構

築」，そして「成果管理を通じた未来の構築　対　社会的使命」という5項目であった。イノベーションは21世紀に向けた将来の発展を導く主要な要素と考えられる。アメリカ，イギリス，およびオーストラリア政府の調査によれば，博物館の役割は，教育，文化，芸術，イノベーション，社会発展，および経済発展と相関関係にあることが明らかとなっている。社会科の知識は，社会的および経済的発展に向けたイノベーションの促進に広く影響を与えるであろう。

ミュージアム2.0：ソーシャルメディアを通じたサイバー空間での拡張展示
【デジタル化および変更管理の観点】

　第3章は，アルメニアのエレバンで開催されたICOM CECA 2012で発表したものである。CECAの会議で「ミュージアム2.0」という概念と「ソーシャルメディアの影響」を発表したのは筆者が初めてであった。

　社会発展の主な推進要因として一般的に挙げられるのは，政治，経済，知識，メディアである。現在は古い産業社会の時代から新しい情報社会の時代への移行期にあり，ソーシャルメディア，デジタルモビリティ，そしてクラウドコンピューティングが人々の考え方や働き方を変えつつある。

　筑波大学教授の水嶋英治が提唱した博物館5世代理論は，博物館の発展に関するまったく新しい説明であった。第1世代は収集，第2世代は保存，第3世代はコミュニケーション（展示と教育），第4世代はインプット／アウトプットに向けたデジタル化，そして第5世代は参加のためのコンバーターという役割を担う，という論説である。

　現在のクラウドコンピューティングやソーシャルメディアの発展を踏まえて，筆者は第6世代の博物館の時代が到来したと考えている。第6世代の博物館とは，文化財の統合と管理のための卓越した中心的存在である。

　プロセスオーナーシップという視点から第6世代博物館を研究すると，これからの博物館に生じる変化のプロセスオーナーが明らかとなる。従来の博物館学芸員たちは，変化と発展のための主要な取り組みや活動をリードする存在であった。ソーシャルメディアは，物理的博物館およびデジタル博物館で人々が見たいものに影響を与えるだけでなく，一般の人々が情報を入手する方法やそ

の情報を知識へと変える方法にまで影響を与える可能性がある。

　博物館を良知，知恵，芸術の展示を通して文明を解釈する知識の源と見なすことは，世界的に新たな傾向となっている。ソーシャルメディアの影響によって，情報化時代における博物館の教育職員は非常に大きな課題に直面しているのである。

栄光と夢：サイバー空間時代における博物館の社会的使命の再考
【第三次産業革命という観点】

　第4章は，第三次産業革命と博物館の関係を論じた。20世紀初頭，農場の仕事は機械化され，農業労働の必要性は低下した。その数十年後には，製造の仕事が機械化され，工場労働の必要性も低下した。現在，サービス部門の多くのビジネスプロセスが機械化されつつあり，必要とされる人員が減少することで体系的な雇用削減という圧力が生じている。

　21世紀の主要な成長原動力のひとつとして，セカンド・エコノミーは多くの雇用機会を生み出すことなしに繁栄を生み出している。今日の社会は，繁栄を生み出す代わりにいかにして分配するかという大きな課題に直面している。従来の共通認識のとおり，富は仕事と関連しているべきである。農業の仕事が段階的に縮小した時点で，世の中には製造の仕事が創出された。さらに，ブルーカラーの製造業が縮小し，ホワイトカラーのサービス業が拡大した。そしてデジタル社会への移行によって，こうしたサービス業も縮小しつつある。将来的にホワイトカラーのビジネスプロセスを伴う雇用は減少すると考えられるため，私たちは問題に直面しているのである。

　筆者は，過去30年間に他の先進工業国が「筋肉系」の構築から「神経系」の開発へと変化している間に，日本で何が生じていたかを探ってきた。その筋肉系を構築する上で，日本はトヨタに代表される多くの一流ブランドを製造業の世界的な主役として確立した。アメリカ人でさえも，技術とイノベーションだけでなく，そのマネジメントシステムまでトヨタから学んでいる。しかし，今後も日本が従来どおりの優位を保てるかという点については疑問が残る。日本は情報通信技術（ICT）の牽引役だった。日本がアメリカの「アップル」に

対抗するためには，韓国におけるサムスンのように，自国の「アップル」を生み出す必要が生じている。最近，ソニーとパナソニックの信用格付けが投機的水準にまで引き下げられたことからも，イノベーションにおける日本の指導的立場が急速に悪化していることがわかる。

　産業の時代にあって，日本はトヨタに代表される強力な「筋肉系」を構築したが，これからは，情報社会へと移行する中で，ソニーやパナソニックのような会社を通じて過去の栄光を再構築し，強力な「神経系」を実現することであろう。

博物館，図書館，アーカブズを変容させる触媒としてのデジタルエンゲージメント：フィールド自然史博物館の事例研究【アメリカの成功事例】
　続く第5章は，日本ミュージアム・マネジメント学会の2017年版研究紀要の招聘論文である。筆者はアメリカ・シカゴ市にある自然史博物館のケーススタディを用いて，博物館の社会的使命と社会サービスの役割の成功事例を提示した。

　シカゴのフィールド自然史博物館は，世界最大の自然史博物館のひとつであり，その教育・科学プログラムの規模と質によって，最高の自然史博物館としての地位を維持している。フィールド博物館自体は，8,000平方メートルの建物スペースを占有するMLAが一体となった施設であり，その収集センターには2,470万点の標本があり，毎年20万点が追加されている。図書館には書籍27万5,000冊，国内外の新聞雑誌278誌，記録資料1,800フィート，希少本7,500冊，芸術作品3,000点が所蔵されている。写真アーカイブは30万枚におよぶ。フィールド博物館には800〜900名の客員教授と研究者がおり，毎年世界中から200万人が訪れている。

　フィールド博物館と同様の事例は他にもある。こうした現象は，アメリカの政治的，経済的，文化的な土壌に根ざしている。アメリカには12万3,000館の図書館と1万7,500館の博物館がある。連邦政府機関である博物館・図書館サービス機構（IMLS）は，図書館や博物館が，助成金，研究，政策展開，および国家的パートナーシップを通じて，イノベーション，生涯学習，そして市

民の文化活動への参加を促進するよう奨励している。博物館や図書館が魅力的な学習体験を提供できるよう支援し，強力なコミュニティアンカーとしての地位を確立させ，そのコレクション管理を支援し，コンテンツへのアクセスを増すためにテクノロジーの活用を推進しているのである。

　フィールド博物館，科学産業博物館，シカゴ美術館，シカゴ中央図書館，およびシカゴ国立公文書館は世界的な機関であり，博物館や図書館の革新と変化をリードしていることを本章では示した。

情報科学による市民のエンパワーメント：サイバー空間における博物館，図書館，アーカブズ【博物館と図書館が公共サービスを提供するにあたっての最大の目標】

　最後の第6章は，ブラジルの『博物館学と文化遺産』研究紀要の論文である。過去20年のサイバー空間における発展と革新は，私たちのライフスタイル，働き方，そして考え方を変革している。iPhoneなどの「スマート」デバイスによって，MLA（博物館，図書館，アーカイブズ）の施設を訪れる前，最中，後における情報の検索と共有が容易になっている。

　博物館が情報技術の波に対処するにあたっての課題に立ち向かう際に役立つよう，地域社会の発展を促す目的で行われてきた成人教育の歴史から教訓が引き出されている。アメリカでは，21世紀型スキルを養成するための教育政策が，MLA部門の社会的使命に及ぼす影響が検討されている。

　将来に向けて世界的に競争力のある人材を育成するために，「P21」（21世紀型スキルのためのパートナーシップ）計画では，アメリカの教室内の環境と実世界の環境とをうまく調和させるための根幹として「3R」と「4C」を特定している。

　3R（読み，書き，算数）には，英語，読書または言語技術，数学，科学，外国語，公民，政治学，経済，芸術，歴史，地理が含まれる。4Cには，批判的思考と問題解決，コミュニケーションとコラボレーション，および創造力とイノベーションが含まれる。3Rが他の科目やコアコンテンツを保護する力として役立つのに対して，4Cには，学業や職業，そして人生における成功に必

要とされるあらゆるスキルが集約されているのである。

　21世紀には，市民は余暇を楽しみ，自分の専門領域を発展させるため生涯学習プログラムに参画することができる。MLAはより一層観衆を開発し，来館者へのより良いサービスを焦点化することになる。MLAの潜在的な観衆はますます多くの情報をもつ一方で，余暇と学習機会の間にある多数のチャネルを選択しなければならない。ということは，MLAへの一般市民参加の増加は，競争の激化により挑発されているのである。MLAは自館の社会的使命の責任を果たすために，有意義で思い出深い文脈の中に彼らが提供するプログラムを位置づける必要がある。

　本書の目的は，情報科学による市民のエンパワーメントおよび生涯学習について筆者自身が学んだことを読者と共有するためである。博物館や図書館，生涯学習機関に属する教育の専門家，および医療促進団体などの非営利団体に対して，市民に生涯学習を促すにあたっての既成の枠組みにとらわれない考え方を提供できるものと考えている。

注・引用文献
1：National Commission on Excellence in Education (1983). *A Nation at Risk*, Washington D. C., the U. S. Department of Education, p. 9. <https://files.eric.ed.gov/fulltext/ED226006.pdf>
　（アメリカ政府電子出版物）
2：チャールズ・ディケンズ，加賀山卓朗（訳）(1859).『二都物語』新潮社, p. 31.

第1章

地域遺産に立脚した良知主導型文化の構築
21世紀における博物館の社会的使命

　世界的に著名な社会学者・費孝通（Fei Xiaotong）は，「すべての国が自国の遺産の価値を重視し，他国の遺産の価値を尊重し，遺産の価値をあらゆる者と共有する日は，世界が平和となる日である」[1]と述べている。これは，1990年12月に，中根千枝教授がこの社会学者のために主催した東京での誕生パーティーでの発言である。歴史的出来事が繰り返されることに驚きを禁じ得ない。というのも，約20年後，ここに集った私たちは，メインテーマである「博物館の中核的な価値の再考と地域遺産」を通して，費と中根が提示したのとまさに同じビジョンを共有しているからである。

　地域遺産に立脚した良知主導型文化の構築は，21世紀における博物館の歴史的・社会的使命となっている。金融市場の失敗が私たちの社会に与えた影響を理解しようとするとき，良知に基づく基本的価値観の欠如がいかにこの悲劇の主な原因のひとつとなったかは容易に理解できる。以下の引用は，私たちがこの問題についての大局観を得る助けとなるであろう。

　　美があまねく美として認められると，そこに醜さがでてくる。
　　善があまねく善として認められると，そこに不善がでてくる。
　　　――老子（老子道徳経　上篇）[2]

　　他人の幸福を願う人は，すでに自分の幸福を手に入れている。
　　　――孔子[3]

第 1 章 地域遺産に立脚した良知主導型文化の構築

これが八正道，すなわち正見，正思惟，正語，正業，正命，正精進，正念，正定である。

如来（仏陀）は中道によって悟りを得たのであるが，この中道は識見，英知，平和，知識，悟り，涅槃に至る道である。

――仏陀（釈迦）ベナレスでの説法[4]

費と中根が提示したビジョンの実現は簡単ではない。インターネットと情報技術は，従来の学習方法を変えただけでなく，私たちの基本的な価値観に影響を与えた。今日，私たちの価値観は，エンターテインメント性と利便性を重視する，商業化されたメディアや情報源によって形づくられている。政府や企業の取り組みを通じて，天然資源の開発には多くの注意が払われてきたが，人的資源の開発はさほど重視されてこなかった。人材育成に注力する国家は，十分な天然資源がなくとも大きな経済的成功を収めることができる。コアバリューの創造に加えて，経済発展のために最新の技術を適用する方法を模索することは，今日の世界文明の重要な使命となっている。

現在，私たちはグローバリゼーションの時代に生きている。周知のとおり，地域ごとにナショナリズムや宗教，利己主義が複雑に絡み合うことから，政治や経済といった文化以外の要素を異文化コミュニケーションの架け橋として使うことは非常に困難である。文化は，世代を超えた価値観を浸透させるための重要な道筋となり得る。文化は本質的に無形であるため，その振興は容易ではないが，美術館のネットワークが，過去，現在，未来を繋ぎ，自国と他国の良知を繋ぐ有形な方法となり得るであろう。

国際良知の場連合（International Coalition of Sites of Conscience）は，21 世紀において博物館の社会的使命をどのように果たしていくかを見直すための好例である。この組織は多くの国の史跡博物館が参加するネットワークであり，以下をポリシーとして掲げている。

史跡の歴史と現代におけるその意味との関わりを一般市民が見いだす手助けをすることは，史跡が果たすべき義務である。私たちは，社会的課題を

強調して対話を促進すること，および人道的・民主主義的価値を促進することを主な役割と位置づけている[5]。

一般市民の社会的責任に関する意識を高めるため，博物館に代表される非営利団体を発展させる必要がある。倫理，道徳，良知，高潔さ，そして人格の教育は，文化に影響を与えると考えられ，その文化が最終的には世界の文明を変える。博物館の専門家として，私たちがこれまでに行ったことやその首尾についてはそれほど重要ではない。しかし，それを行ったことの必要性を知ることは非常に重要である。

一般的に，博物館の主な機能としては，調査研究，収集，保存，展示，教育などがあると考えられている。Wikipediaにも記されているが，「博物館」という言葉は，ミューズ（ギリシア神話で芸術を司る神）に捧げられた場所または寺院を表すラテン語に由来し，したがって研究と芸術のための建物，特に哲学や研究のためのMuseum（研究所）を指す。

私たちが直面している第一の課題は，博物館に対する一般認識を「観光名所」から「地域遺産の源泉」へといかに変えるかという点，そしてその保全と振興である。一般市民は博物館の真の価値を理解することがなければ，がっかりさせられてしまうであろう。これは，地域社会やビジネスリーダー，教育関係者，政府関係者，政治家など，一般市民の利害関係者にとって深刻な問題となっている。つい先頃，中国政府は，一般市民が入場しやすくなるよう，主要な国立博物館や地域博物館の入場料を段階的に引き下げた。しかし，博物館の専門家のトレーニングは不十分で，来館者に博物館の価値を適切に教える方法についての情報はほとんどない。

第二の課題は，博物館の専門家がナレッジブローカーとして地域遺産に基づく良知主導の文化を構築するための体系的なアプローチをいかに生み出すかという点である。

博物館を知識仲介の場としてとらえるには，知識仲介を展開するすべての段階をカバーするために，全面的なエンド・ツー・エンドのプロセスを導入する必要がある。このプロセスは，知識の創造，獲得，同化，使用，普及の各段階

に分けることができる。

　バックエンドの研究・サポートスタッフおよび来館者に対応する学習・開発スタッフの専門的な育成が急務である。加盟博物館の協力のもと，知識仲介プロセスに向けた，規格化されたプロセス，方法論，そして認定を伴うカリキュラムやワークショップを開発することは，ICOM-ASPAC（アジア太平洋連盟）にとって大きなイニシアチブとなり得る。

　結論的にいえば，世界平和を生み出すために地域遺産を保護することの重要性をあらゆる利害関係者に理解させるには，国境を越えた包括的な官民パートナーシップを構築するべきである。博物館は，体系的なアプローチを用いることで，21世紀における社会的使命を果たす手段として知識仲介のシステムを発展させることが可能となるだろう。その使命とは，自国に固有な遺産を継承しつつ，同時に他国の遺産とも融合させることである，と指摘できる。

注・引用文献
1：費孝通（2013），全球化与文化自觉：費孝通晚年文选，北京，外语教学与研究出版社，p. 6-16.
　　本書には正式な英文翻訳はない。
2：Lin YuTang（2009）. *Chinese-English Bilingual Edition: The Wisdom of Laotse (1)*（Bilingual literature, Volume 1），Taipei, Cheng Chung Book Co., Ltd; 2nd edition（2009），p. 60.
3：Bell, D.（2000）. *East Meets West: Human Rights and Democracy in East Asia*, Princeton University Press, p. 244.
4：Price, J.（2010）. *Sacred Scriptures of the World Religions: An Introduction*, Bloomsbury Academic, p. 58.
5：The International Coalition of Sites of Conscience <www.sitesofconscience.org>

第2章

博物館建設における課題と好機
日中の比較による歴史的・社会的見地から

　2010年現在，中国は30年にわたる自由貿易政策により，日本を追い越して世界第2位の経済大国となっている。同時に，中国における博物館数は，1978年の300館から2010年には3,000館に増加した。日本では1945年の145館から2003年には5,000館へと増加している。日中のさまざまな経済発展段階において博物館が担った公共サービスの役割を歴史比較方法論に基づいて研究することで，地域経済の成長を通した文化の発展の影響に関する新たな展望が明らかになると期待できる。日中を比較する際の主な特徴点は以下5項目である。

1. 政府主導　対　学術団体主導
2. 公教育を通じた経済成長　対　大衆政治運動
3. ランドマークの開発を通した成熟　対　文化遺産の保護
4. 博物館の病変から生じる神話　対　ハードウェアの構築
5. 成果管理を通じた未来の構築　対　社会的使命

　Rostow（1960）が提唱した産業化への5段階ロードマップ（経済発展段階説）を，Porter（2002）が改良したS字カーブ理論で検討することで，イノベーションは21世紀に向けた将来の発展を導く主要な要素とされた。アメリカ，イギリス，およびオーストラリア政府の調査によれば，博物館の役割は，教育，文化芸術，イノベーション，社会発展，および経済発展と相関関係にあることが明らかとなっている。社会科の知識は，社会的および経済的発展に向けたイノベーションの促進に広く影響を与えるであろう。

第 2 章　博物館建設における課題と好機

2.1　背景：日中の奇跡的な経済発展

　2011 年 7 月に世界銀行が発表した 2010 年の国内総生産（GDP）に関する世界開発指標データベースによると，中国の GDP は 5 兆 8,786 億 2,900 万ドル，日本の GDP は 5 兆 4,978 億 1,300 万ドルであった。過去 30 年にわたる自由貿易政策により，中国は 2010 年に日本を抜いて世界第 2 位の経済大国となった。図 1 は，過去 20 年間の日本と中国における GDP 成長の推移を示している。

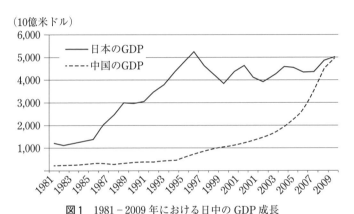

図 1　1981 – 2009 年における日中の GDP 成長
出典：世界銀行の Web サイト掲載のデータ[1]をもとに著者作成

　中国は現在，本当に日本を上回ったのだろうか。表 1 からは，中国がいかに日本に遅れているかが読み取れる。とはいえ，文化，遺産，および社会的・経済的発展について，両国間には多くの類似点がある。日本がその社会発展のさまざまな段階で学んだ教訓を研究することは，中国の発展の道筋に役立つと考えられる。Wang（2006）の研究によれば，中国は膨大な人口と天然資源の不足だけでなく，博愛のための資源の不足に起因する深刻な課題に直面しており，これらが持続可能な発展に大きな障害を引き起こしている。社会の基本的価値と中国の文化遺産について再考することは，調和的社会の構築に貢献する 2 つの重要な道筋になるだろう。

表 1　日中の経済比較

	日本	中国
人口（単位：百万人）	126	1,336
都市部人口（2010 年）	67 %	47 %
都市化率（2010-2015 年）	0.2 %	2.3 %
面積（km²）	377,915	9,596,961
GDP（単位：兆　米ドル，2010 年）	5,497	5,878
成長率（%）	3.9 %	10.3 %
一人当たりの GDP（単位：米ドル，2010 年）	34,000	7,600
部門別 GDP		
農業	1.4 %	10.2 %
工業	24.9 %	46.9 %
サービス業	73.8 %	43.0 %
労働力人口（単位：百万人，2010 年）	63	815
部門別労働力人口		
農業	3.9 %	38.1 %
工業	26.2 %	27.8 %
サービス業	69.8 %	34.1 %

出典：CIA（2011）．The World Factbook[2]

　過去 20 年間に，中国の博物館部門は，国家経済の高い成長率とともに急速に成長してきた。図 2 は，日中の博物館の数と比較した GDP 成長率の傾向を示している。両国で GDP も博物館も同様の成長傾向にあることから，この現象を量的・質的分析を通じて研究することで，21 世紀に向けた博物館建設の課題と好機を理解しようと試みた。

　第 12 次 5 カ年計画（2011-2015 年）により，中国の博物館数は 3,500 館に増加した。これは 4 年間で 150〜180 館の博物館が新設されたことを意味する（国家文物局，2011）。本研究では，歴史社会学的研究と文化経済学を組み合わせた方法論を用いて，日中の博物館建設に向けた課題と好機を理解する。

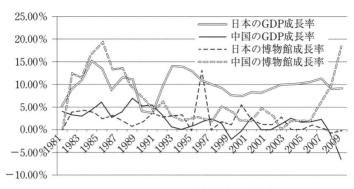

図 2　日中における GDP と博物館の成長率
出典：世界銀行（GDP）[3]，文部科学省「博物館の振興」[4]，国家文物局（中国の博物館）[5] をもとに筆者作成

2.2　博物館の社会的使命

　博物館を，良知，知恵，そして芸術の展示を通して，人類文明を解釈する「知識の源」と見なすことは，国際的な新しい傾向である（Wang, 2009）。2007年にウィーンで採択された国際博物館会議（ICOM）規約によれば，博物館は「社会とその発展に貢献し，教育，研究，娯楽のために人間とその環境の有形，無形の文化遺産を収集，保存，調査研究，伝達，展示を行う公衆に開かれた非営利の常設機関である」[6] と定義されている。

　ICOM 規約は当初，「収蔵」に重点を置いて作成されたが，ほどなく 1951 年には「保存，研究，向上」を含むよう修正された。教育機能は 1961 年に追加され，社会とその発展に貢献するという項目は 1974 年に追加された。1989 年，1995 年，2001 年にも博物館の定義は拡大されてきた。2007 年には，「研究と楽しみ」を超えて「教育」が博物館の基本的業務における最優先の共通目的とされた。

　このように博物館の定義が活発に発展するのに伴い，国際的な博物館界は調和的社会を築くための社会的使命を積極的に主張し，追求している。2009 年に東京で開催された国際博物館会議　アジア太平洋地域（ICOM-ASPAC）の

テーマは「アジア太平洋地域における博物館の中核的な価値の再考と地域遺産」であり，2010年に上海で行われたICOM大会のテーマは「博物館と社会的調和」であった。

2.3 博物館，イノベーション，そして持続可能な社会発展

2006年にはロンドン・スクール・オブ・エコノミクスの教授Tony Travers が，イギリス博物館・図書館・文書館国家評議会（MLA）およびイギリスNMDC（National Museums Directors Conference）の依頼を受けて調査を行った。その報告書では，イギリスの主要博物館・美術館の数多い経済的・社会的影響に関する最新の分析が提示された。博物館は，社会の中で都市の発展と経済再生を促進する上で主導的な役割を果たした。Travers は，「イギリスの博物館や美術館は，さらなる拡大と改善の余地があり，この国が創造性と学問の世界的リーダーとなる原動力たりうる」[7]と指摘している。報告書の肯定的な所見としては，以下の内容が挙げられる。

- イギリスの主要博物館・美術館の経済的利益は，取引高と来館者の支出を考慮して，年間15億ポンドと推定される。広範な経済効果はさらに大きいだろう。
- 概して，イギリス経済の1,000ポンドあたり1ポンドは博物館と美術館部門に直接起因するものである。[8]

Cutler（2008）は，イノベーションに関する研究を通じて，文化芸術を経済発展と明確に結びつけた。そしてイノベーション・産業・科学・研究省に対する報告書「冒険するオーストラリア：イノベーションにおける力の構築」の中で，文化と芸術の自己認識と公的なイノベーションの枠組みや政策，プログラムとの間に大きな隔たりがあったことを指摘した。202ページにわたる同報告書は，他の先進国を研究しただけでなく，中国やインドなどの新興国にも注目した。Cutlerは，イノベーションが21世紀の重要な原動力のひとつであると

確信し,「すべてのオーストラリア人の中にイノベーション精神を育むべきである。イノベーション精神を育むことができれば,オーストラリアは,進取的で冒険的な国となれるだろう」[9]と指摘している。

アメリカでは早くも1983年から,教育が国の競争力を維持する鍵であることを認識していた。教育の卓越性に関する国家委員会(The National Commission of Excellence in Education)の報告書「危機に立つ国家」には,「今日の社会の教育基盤は,国家・国民としての未来を脅かす凡庸さの潮流によって侵食されつつある(中略)かつては商業,産業,科学,技術革新の卓越性を誇り確固たる地位を築いていたアメリカが,世界中の競争相手に追い越されつつある。問題の原因や規模はさまざまだが,教育はアメリカの繁栄,安全,そして礼節を支える要素である」[10]と記されている。高校教育の基本的スキルとして,英語,数学,科学,社会,コンピューターサイエンスの5科目を挙げ,「科学技術を創造的かつ人間味のあるものとし続けるためには,人類が維持してきた人文科学の知識をこれに役立てなければならない」[11]と明言している。

Rostow(1960)は,国が産業化する過程を説明するためのロードマップとして5段階モデルを作成した。これらの5段階とは,次のとおりである[12]。

1. 伝統的な社会
2. 離陸先行期
3. 経済的離陸
4. 成熟化
5. 大量消費の時代

このモデルは,イギリス,アメリカ,カナダ,日本などほとんどの先進国にあてはめることができるであろう。今日,第三次産業と第四次産業は,21世紀の経済発展を牽引する2つの主要部門となっているが,そのいずれもが知識集約型であり,主要な動輪としてイノベーションが必要とされているのである。

2.4 日本と中国から学ぶこと

歴史社会学的方法論の適用によって，日本と中国における，経済発展と対比させた博物館建設の歴史を，時代と地域別に調査した。この歴史比較研究のためには，質的・量的手法を組み合わせた。ここでの目的は，時代，国民，地域社会，および社会・経済発展などの要素を用いて，教育とイノベーションにおける博物館の役割を理解することである。

比較を容易にするために，5段階のアプローチを設けて，日本が他の先進国と同様の問題に対処するにあたり，いかに博物館を利用して社会教育制度を発展させたかを明らかにするとともに，中国が高度経済成長とともにいかに博物館制度を発展させたかを把握したい。

段階Ⅰ：近代的博物館の創設

日本（1861－1950年）：日本の運営モデルは「行政主導」であった。日本政府は，国有資産，天然資源，生産物や農産物を管理する必要性，および外国貿易や産業開発に関する国家政策に向けた産業情報収集の必要性から，全国的な博物館の設立を開始した。日本の博物館は社会経済発展のためという「DNA」をもって誕生したのである。1936年には，韓国と台湾それぞれ10館を含む320館の博物館が設立された。

中国（1905－1936年）：中国の運営モデルは「学術団体主導」であった。学界は，新たな文化運動の中で，科学と民主主義のニーズに応えるために博物館を立ち上げた。学会会議録を備えた中国博物館協会は1936年に設立された。中国の博物館は文化的・学術的発展のためという「DNA」を持って生まれたのである。1936年には，紫禁城博物館を含む77館の博物館が設立された。

段階Ⅱ：地域社会教育のプラットフォーム

日本（1950－1969年）：博物館が担った主な役割は，社会経済の発展に伴う

社会教育であった。1950年，1951年には教育法，社会教育法，博物館法，理科教育振興法，産業教育振興法が制定された。Teuchi（2010）によれば，公民館，図書館，博物館は日本の社会教育制度を支える3本柱となった。日本は，経済および社会の高度成長を経験し，1965年から1977年にかけて1,670館の博物館が新たに開館した。

中国（1949 - 1976年）：博物館は国家政策教育のプラットフォームとなった。博物館が担った主な役割は，社会主義教育を伴う政治宣伝であった。博物館の建物や運営，基準，建築，および展示デザインは，旧ソビエト連邦のモデルに沿って開発され，政治運動の影響を強く受けた同国に全面的に倣ったものだった。博物館の主な焦点は「階級闘争」に置かれた。1966年から1976年にかけての文化革命によって，社会と文化は大きく損なわれた。1976年の博物館数は72館であった。

段階Ⅲ：国家改革による成長

日本（1969 - 1989年）：日本は明治維新から100周年となる1968年にGDP世界第2位の経済大国となり，社会経済発展の頂点に達した。「地方」「文化」「グローバリゼーション」は，地方自治体による新しい博物館建設のテーマとなった。企業の記念博物館やアートギャラリーも，博物館建設におけるもうひとつの社会的トレンドとなり，地域社会の発展において「企業文化」が流行語となった。中央政府，地方自治体，そして大企業が年に150館の博物館を新設し，博物館の数は1977年に3,289館に達した。

中国（1978 - 1990年）：鄧小平の自由貿易政策は，「中国博物館の新たな春」をもたらした。以降，社会的および政治的な一連の出来事が中国を変えた。文化遺産の保存に重点的に取り組むことが，博物館建設の重要な視点となった。中央政府と地方自治体によって，年間100〜120館の博物館が新設された。中国初の現代博物館である陝西歴史博物館は，計画から完成までに8年を要した（1983 - 1991年）。

段階Ⅳ：博物館建設の見直し

　日本（1990－2000年）：200館の博物館が中央政府，地方自治体，およびコミュニティによって設立された。博物館建設の絶頂期にあって，博物館のビジョンとミッション管理は見失われた。こうした博物館の病的状況を経て，日本博物館協会は改革のために成すべきことを認識するに至った。「メセナ」（企業による芸術活動の支援）によって，博物館および芸術振興のための支援，奨励，または財政援助に向けた官民パートナーシップ（PPP）が導入された。一般市民は，21世紀に備えるための生涯学習を意識し始めた。

　中国（1990－2010年）：都市開発のランドマークやシンボルとして，年間100〜120館の博物館が，中央政府および地方自治体によって新設された。不動産主導型の経済によって，博物館は都市化の一部に組み込まれ，その社会的使命と公共サービス機能に関してはほとんど考慮されなかった。ハードウェアの構築が唯一の論点となり，新たな課題が生まれることとなった。中国は，同様の「ハードウェア」問題における日本の足跡をたどったのである。

段階Ⅴ：目的主導型のマネジメント

　日本（2000年－　）：日本ミュージアム・マネジメント学会（JMMA）は博物館評価のための格付けシステムを開発した。バランススコアカード（BSC）等の各種方法論を用いてパフォーマンス管理が導入されたほか，市民参加型社会教育に向けたデジタル化，対話，そしてコミュニケーションが提唱された。2002年の教育改革により，高校生の社会教育の一環として総合学習の時間が設けられた。

　中国（2011年－　）：中国の遺産を保護し，公衆共有の心のふるさとを築くことが国家の使命とされた。中央政府，地方自治体，および個人投資家によって年間200〜220館の博物館が新設される予定である。中国の指導者は博物館の社会的使命と公共サービスの役割を再検討しつつある。イノベーション国

家，持続可能な経済，環境に配慮した発展，および文化の発展が，博物館建設の新たな観点となっている。博物館による社会教育は徐々に評価されつつある。

　日本は，社会的使命に沿って博物館を開発するための運営の仕組みにおいて，中国に先んじている。文化遺産の保護と公衆共有の心のふるさとの建設は，中国の博物館部門の社会的使命となっている。日中ともに，現在においても改善と卓越性を追求し続けている。

2.5　結語

　21 世紀の社会発展のためには，博物館が社会的使命として自らの公共サービス機能を強化しようと検討することが大きな課題と好機となっている。文化遺産を保護し，世界最高レベルのベストプラクティスを適用して心のふるさとを築くことは，博物館に携わる者たちの歴史的使命である。過去 30 年の間に，先進国は博物館の社会的使命と公共サービスを国民の生涯学習の支援および学習社会構築というカテゴリーに組み込んできた。たとえば，日本にある 5,600 館の博物館は，公民館，図書館とともに国民の生涯学習体系を支える 3 本柱のひとつとなっている。日本は，欧米のベストプラクティスを取り入れることにより，学習社会の創造に向けてアジア文化の特徴のある国民生涯学習体系を開発してきた。これに伴い，博物館法，社会教育法，図書館法，生涯学習振興法などの教育関連法が制定されている。

　中国の博物館の発展過程については，国際社会（特に日本）と非常に多くの類似点がある。国家文化財総局が公表したデータによると，中国の博物館数は 1949 年の 24 館から 2010 年には 3,000 館以上に増加している。中国は，博物館の公共サービス機能を国民の生涯学習を支援するために取り入れることによって，他の国々との大きな差を埋めなければならない。中国は，社会発展に寄与するための博物館の発展に関して，法的枠組み，運営体制，管理システム，人材養成の面でまだ国際水準から大きく遅れをとっている。

表2 日中の博物館制度の発展

段階	博物館制度の発展	日本	中国
I	近代的博物館の創設	1861 – 1950	1905 – 1936
II	地域社会教育のプラットフォーム	1950 – 1969	1949 – 1976
III	国家改革による成長	1969 – 1989	1978 – 1990
IV	博物館建設の見直し	1990 – 2000	1990 – 2010
V	目的主導型のマネジメント	2000 –	2011 –

注・引用文献
1：The WORLD BANK. GDP <https://data.worldbank.org/indicator/NY.GDP.MKTP.CD>
2：CIA (2011). The World Factbook <https://www.cia.gov/library/publications/the-world-factbook/>
3：The WORLD BANK. GDP <https://data.worldbank.org/indicator/NY.GDP.MKTP.CD>
4：文部科学省 (2011). 博物館の振興 <http://www.mext.go.jp/a_menu/01_l/08052911/1313126.htm>
5：ここで用いたテータは中国政府関係資料と中国文化遺産管理局のデータをもとにしている。中国の正式な資料は限定されているため，さまざまな報道関係資料も参考とした。
6：ICOM Statutes, Approved in Vienna (Austria) August 24, 2007, p. 2. <http://icom.museum/fileadmin/user_upload/pdf/Statuts/statutes_eng.pdf>
7：Travers (2006). Museums and Galleries in Britain: Economic, social and creative impacts, London, National Museum Directors' Conference, p. 6. <http://www.nationalmuseums.org.uk/media/documents/publications/museums_galleries_in_britain_travers_2006.pdf>
8：ibid., p. 16.
9：Cutler (2008). Report: Venturous Australia–Building Strength in Innovation, Sydney, Ministry for Innovation, Industry, Science and Research, p. viii. <http://www.innovation.gov.au/Innovation/Policy/Documents/NISReport.pdf>
10：National Commission on Excellence in Education (1983). *A Nation at Risk,*

Washington D. C., the U. S. Department of Education, p. 9. <https://files.eric.ed.gov/fulltext/ED226006.pdf>

11 : ibid., p. 9.

12 : Rostow (1960). *The Stages of Economic Growth: A Non-Communist Manifesto,* Cambridge, Cambridge University Press, p. 4.

参考文献

CIA (2011). The World Factbook <https://www.cia.gov/library/publications/the-world-factbook/>

Cutler (2008). Report: Venturous Australia-Building Strength in Innovation, Sydney, Ministry for Innovation, Industry, Science and Research <http://www.innovation.gov.au/Innovation/Policy/Documents/NISReport.pdf>

Jan-Yen Huang (2005). From the Age of "Cultural Affairs as Administration" to the Age of "Culture Enterprise for the Public": A Critical Study of the Meaning and Challenge of the Administrative Corporation in National Museums in Taiwan, and Comparison with the Japan Experience, Taipei, *Museology Quarterly* *.

National Commission on Excellence in Education (1983), *A Nation at Risk,* Washington D. C., the U. S. Department of Education.

Porter (2002). *The Global Competitiveness Report 2001-2002,* New York, Oxford University Press.

Rostow (1960). *The Stages of Economic Growth: A Non-Communist Manifesto,* Cambridge, Cambridge University Press.

Teuchi, Akitoshi (2010). Japanese Education System and Practice, Tokyo, Center for Research on International Cooperation in Educational Development (CRICED), University of Tsukuba.

Travers (2006). Museums and Galleries in Britain: Economic, social and creative impacts, London, National Museum Directors' Conference <http://www.nationalmuseums.org.uk/media/documents/publications/museums_galleries_in_britain_travers_2006.pdf>

Travers and Glaister (2004). Valuing Museums: Impact and Innovation Among National Museums, London, National Museum Directors' Conference <http://www.national-museums.org.uk/media/documents/publications/valuing_museums.pdf>

Wang, L. (2009). "Building Conscience Driven Culture by Regional Heritage - Social Mission of Museums for the 21st Century," Proceeding of ICOM ASPAC TOKYO, 2009.

Wang, W. (2006). "Scientific Outlook: Concept and Practice," Beijing, Central Party School Press.

World Bank (2011). World Development Indicators database <http://siteresources.worldbank.org/DATASTATISTICS/Resources/GDP.pdf>

*博物館学季刊誌は台湾国立中央図書館の「台灣人文及社會科學引文索引資料庫（TCIHSS）」から検索可能である。

第3章

ミュージアム 2.0
ソーシャルメディアによるサイバー空間での拡張展示

　Dippel（2002）は，社会発展の主な推進要因として政治，経済，知識，メディアを挙げている。数名の著名な社会学者は早くも 1970 年から，将来の傾向を予測していた。現在私たちは古い産業社会の時代から新しい情報社会の時代への移行期にある。今日，ソーシャルメディア，デジタルモビリティ，そしてクラウドコンピューティングが人々の考え方や働き方を変えつつある。過去 30 年間に，博物館という分野にどのような変化が生じたのだろうか。博物館の専門家として，私たちは社会の変化に対応する用意があるだろうか。

　Toffler（1980）は，文化と地域社会の発展を表す「第三の波」理論を生み出した。第一の波は，それまでの狩猟採集民の文化を覆した新石器革命以来，世界の大部分で広く普及した定住農業社会である。第二の波は産業社会であり，産業革命によって西ヨーロッパで始まり，次いで世界中に広がった。第三の波は，脱産業社会である。Toffler は，1950 年代後半以降，ほとんどの国が第二の波の社会から第三の波の社会に移行しつつあると述べている。彼はそれを記述するために多くの言葉を作り出し，「情報化時代」といった他人が発明した造語にも言及している。

　この変化とは何か。産業革命以来，最大の変化だろうか。

　筆者は史上最大といえるほどの変化だと確信している。この変化は無限に続き，無限に広がる。博物館の専門家たちは，これからの博物館がこうした変化について広く国民の認識を高める方法を探ろうと積極的に取り組んできた。水嶋の考える博物館 5 世代理論によると，現在の博物館は第 4 世代であり，第 5 世代に近づきつつある。ちなみに第 1 世代は収集，第 2 世代は保存，第 3 世代

は展示と教育, 第4世代はインプット／アウトプットに向けたデジタル化, そして第5世代は参加のためのコンバーターという役割を担う。

現在のクラウドコンピューティングやソーシャルメディアの発展を踏まえて, 筆者は第6世代の博物館の時代が到来したと考えている。第6世代の博物館とは, 卓越した文化財の統合および管理の中心的存在である。

図1は, 博物館第6世代研究におけるミッション管理の全体像を示している。これからの博物館を変化させていく取り組みにおいて, 鍵となるのは地域社会中心主義である。文化財管理にあたっては, ソーシャルメディアと博物館の使命が, 調和的な社会を構築するという私たちの社会的使命に与える影響を考慮することになろう。

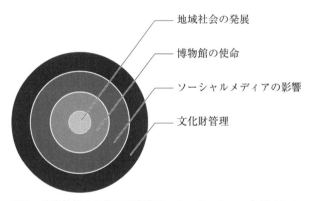

図1 博物館第6世代の研究次元：ミッション・マネジメント

図2は, 博物館第6世代研究におけるプロセスオーナーシップの全体像を示している。これからの博物館に生じる変化のプロセスオーナーは誰になるのだろうか。従来の博物館学芸員たちは, 変化と発展のための主要な取り組みや活動をリードする存在であった。しかしこれはもはや事実とは異なる。ソーシャルメディアは, 物理的博物館およびデジタル博物館で人々が見たいものに影響を与えるだけでなく, 一般の人々が情報を入手する方法やその情報を知識へと変える方法にまで影響を与える可能性がある。

第 3 章　ミュージアム2.0

図 2　博物館第 6 世代の研究次元：プロセスオーナーシップ

　博物館学芸員がソーシャルメディアに対処するには，どうしたらよいのか。ソーシャルメディアが博物館に与える影響については，未だにごく限られた情報しかない。筆者は e ガバメント2.0 をミュージアム2.0 の参考とした。

　デジタル化は人々の働き方やライフスタイルを変えた。Neilson（2009）の報告によると，世界のインターネット人口の 3 分の 2 がソーシャルネットワークやブログサイトを訪問しており，それはインターネット使用時間のほぼ 10 ％を占めている。

　Richardson（2011）は，ソーシャルメディアのトップ 3 である Facebook, Twitter, Klout からデータを入手する方法を生み出し，3,635 館の博物館や美術館を追跡した結果，Facebook 上では 1,186 万 3,882 人の「いいね」を，Twitter 上では 1,290 万 9,649 人の「フォロワー」を発見した。ソーシャルメディアは諸刃の剣である。各博物館には平均 8,000 人のフォロワーがおり，ボランティアとして私たちの日常業務に注意を払い，自分の意見を表明するだけでなく，投票によって私たちの仕事を評価している。水は航行のための水路を作り出すが，一方で船を沈めさせることもある。博物館の専門家は，Facebook, Twitter, YouTube などのソーシャルメディアの幅広い活用に特別な注意を払う必要がある。ソーシャルメディアを通じた「拡張展示（extended exhibition）」と筆者が呼んでいるものは，従来の常設展や臨時展に加えて，社会に

影響を与える新しい方法である。

　博物館や博物館の専門家は，サイバー空間時代にあって情報技術の波を乗りこなす準備ができているだろうか。Dicker（2009）は，オーストラリア，イギリス，アメリカ，ノルウェー，ニュージーランドの計 96 人の学芸員に対して「学芸員の生活にブログその他のソーシャルメディアが及ぼす影響」と題する調査を 2009 年に行った。その結果，博物館学芸員の役割がソーシャルメディアによって大きく影響を受けていることが明らかとなった。学芸員の「エキスパート」「スペシャリスト」としての伝統的な役割は縮小している。研究者やナレッジブローカーという位置づけは，今日の実情を正しく反映するものではない。ソーシャルメディアは新たな意見や新たな票決方法を生み出し，サイバー空間における拡張展示の管理に新しい次元を加える可能性がある。

　技術開発は博物館に新たなプラットフォームを誕生させた。これは博物館の学芸員にどのような影響を与えるだろうか。学芸員はソーシャルメディアをキュレーションの実践に取り入れているだろうか。取り入れている場合，ソーシャルメディアの空間でどのように交流しているのだろうか。そしてこれらすべてが学芸員の役割と彼らが手がける収集コレクションにどのような影響を与えているのだろうか。学芸員は，以前は公開講座やアウトリーチ活動，ウェブサイト編集などのスタッフ業務の領域であった双方向コミュニケーションの需要が増加する中で，さまざまな課題に直面している。学芸員は私生活の中でソーシャルメディアを利用しているだろうか。調査対象者の大半（80.5％）は，ソーシャルメディアを個人的に利用している。最も人気のあるプラットフォームは，Facebook，YouTube，Flickr，MySpace，ブログへのコメントなどである。この他に LinkedIn と nings なども利用されている。個人的な利用のためにサイバー空間に身を置く学芸員は，ネットワーク化されたソーシャルメディアへの参加傾向がより強い。調査参加者全体の 36.7％が職務においてソーシャルメディアを利用していなかった。その理由として圧倒的に多かったのは，ソーシャルメディアの利用には時間がかかり，その時間をもてないというものであった。実際，利用していないと答えた人の 90％が，職場でもっとソーシャルメディアの研修を受けたいと考えていた。

自らが所属する博物館のウェブサイトで，自分がミュージアム 2.0 の時代にいるかどうかをチェックできる。博物館のウェブサイトはミュージアム 1.0 または AOL の時代から進化した。以前の時代には，人々は Google 検索，電子メールやインスタントメッセージの利用，および AOL や Yahoo によって選ばれたコンテンツのチャットルームに参加することで当該博物館を見つけることができた。ウェブサイトは情報源と位置づけられ，博物館のサイトは情報や訪問計画を提供するように設計されていた。ミュージアム 2.0 または Facebook の時代においては，潜在的な来館者はソーシャルネットワークの投稿を通じて当該博物館を見つけることができる。ソーシャルメディアはウェブへの入り口として使用される。会員コミュニティは社会に強い影響を与える。博物館がソーシャルネットワークを利用することは，効果的なマーケティングツールとして非常に重要である。

ミュージアム 2.0 の利用は，ガバメント 2.0 と多くの類似点をもっている。Freeman と Loo（2009）は，政府が Web2.0 の技術を利用することによって，効率性，ユーザーの利便性，市民参画という 3 つのカテゴリーのメリットを得られると示唆している。博物館のウェブサイトは博物館の情報，展示の情報，アクセスと開館時間，および見学プランに関する情報提供に重点を置き，政府のウェブサイトは情報の流布，教育，および観光に重点を置いていた。

Kuzma（2010）はアジア 50 カ国の調査を行い，アジアでは政府のわずか 30 ％しか Web 2.0 ツールを使用していないことを明らかにした。先進国においては，この割合がはるかに高い。アジアの政府の大半は，国民とのコミュニケーションのための効果的なツールとしてのソーシャルメディアの重要性を認識していない。Web 2.0 ツールを活用するための戦略的方向性の欠如が共通の課題となっている。ソーシャルメディアツールに対する，恐怖や懸念を含む複雑な認識は，民主主義運動の発展に影響を与える可能性がある。図 3 は，ガバメント 2.0 の 4 つの適用カテゴリーを示している。ガバメント 2.0 は，e-デモクラシー運動の検閲，インターネットアクセスのない低所得世帯に対する公平性，資金調達の持続可能性と運用の継続性，そして市民のプライバシーと安全保護に特別な注意を払っている。興味深いのは，政府と博物館を置き換えて

も,簡単に同様の結論に達するという点だ。

　博物館を良知,知恵,芸術の展示を通して文明を解釈する知識の源と見なすことは,世界的に新たな傾向となっている。ソーシャルメディアの影響によって,情報化時代における博物館の教育職員は非常に大きな課題に直面している。

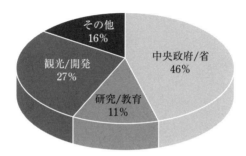

図3　アジアにおけるeガバメント 2.0 の適用状況

参考文献

Dicker (2009). The Impact of Blogs and Other Social Media on the Life of a Curator <http://www.museumsandtheweb.com/mw2010/papers/dicker/dicker.html#ixzz29dRORoyN>

Dippel (2002). *The Language of Conscience,* Brenham, Texas, Texas Peacemaker Publications, LLC.

Freeman and Loo (2009). "Web 2.0 and E-government at the Municipal Level," 5th International Conference on e-Government 2009, Boston, MA, U.S.A.

Kuzma (2010). "Asian Government Usage of Web 2.0 Social Media," European Journal of ePractice <http://www.etudasportal.gov.hu/download/attachments/7995452/European+Journal+epractice+Volume+9.6.pdf>

Nielson (2009). Global Faces and Network Places: A Nelson Report on Social Networking's New Global Footprints, Nielson Company <http://www.nielsen.com/us/en/insights/reports/2009/Social-Networking-New-Global-Footprint.html>

Richardson (2011). The Top 50 - Museums in Social Media <http://litot.es/museums-in-social-media/>

Toffler (1980). *The Third Wave,* New York, U.S.A., William Morrow and Company.

Wang (2011). "Challenges & Opportunities in Museum Development A Historic-Sociological Perspective: China versus Japan," Proceeding of ICOM CECA Zagreb, Croatia.

第4章

栄光と夢
サイバー空間時代における博物館の社会的使命の再考

　2012年秋，筆者は国際博物館会議アジア太平洋地域連盟（ICOM ASPAC）武漢会議に招待され，「サイバー空間時代の博物館：グローバル・ビレッジにおける学際的な次元」と題したスピーチを行った。また，同年にエレバンで開催された国際博物館会議　教育と文化活動委員会（ICOM CECA）では，「ミュージアム2.0：ソーシャルメディアによるサイバー空間における展示の拡大」と題したスピーチを行った。その中のキーワード「サイバー空間」および「ソーシャルメディア」は，いずれの会議でも多数の聴衆に大きなインパクトを与えた。会議の終了後，ソーシャルメディアが博物館の社会的使命と公共サービスに及ぼす影響に関して多くの質問を受けたことで，この問題についていっそう考察を深めることとなった。交換研究者という立場から，日本の博物館の社会的使命と公共サービスに関する歴史的・社会学的研究を他国との比較研究を通じて行うにあたり，既存の枠組みにとらわれずに思考することができた。

4.1　博物館近代化への道

　日本は明治維新100周年となる1968年にGDP世界第2位の経済大国となった。1964年には東京で夏季オリンピックが開催された（10月10日〜24日）。これはアジアで開催された初のオリンピックである。1970年には大阪府吹田市で日本万国博覧会が開催された（3月15日〜9月13日）。「人類の進歩と調和」をテーマに掲げたこの万博は，アジアで初めて開催された万博であり，日本は

栄光に輝いてこの夢を実現したのである。日本はアジアで初めて産業先進国の仲間入りをし，アジアの希望の星となった。日本からは高い品質と革新性を備えた数々の主力ブランドが誕生した。

　日本における近代博物館というものの始まりは，1861年から1951年の期間にさかのぼる。この取り組みは「行政主導」のもとで推し進められた。日本政府は，国有資産，天然資源，生産物を管理する必要性，および外国貿易や産業開発に関する国家政策に向けた情報収集の必要性から，全国的な博物館の設立を開始した。そのため，日本の博物館は社会経済発展の「DNA」をもって誕生したのである。1936年には，韓国と台湾それぞれ10館を含む320館の博物館が設立された。

　調査の視点によっては，1969年から1989年までの期間が博物館発展の黄金期であると考えることができる。明治維新100周年を祝う記念式典とともに，日本は社会・経済発展のピークを迎えた。「地方」「文化」「グローバリゼーション」が，地方自治体が新しい博物館を建設するためのテーマとなった。企業の記念博物館やアートギャラリーも，博物館発展におけるもうひとつの社会的トレンドとなり，地域社会の発展において企業文化が流行語となった。中央政府，地方自治体，そして大企業が年に150館の博物館を新設し，博物館の数は1977年に3,289館に達した。

4.2　メガトレンド

　Naisbitt（1982）の著書『メガトレンド：10の社会潮流が近未来を決定づける』は，世界で1,400万部販売され57カ国でベストセラーとなった。著者は「未来を予測する最も信頼できる方法は現在を理解することである」という研究の原則を採用し，情報社会が以前の産業社会とどのように異なるかに関する自身の長期的な見地から，説得力のある説を展開した。彼が予測した10のメガトレンドは以下のとおりである。

　①産業社会を経て情報社会へ，②強制的に使用されるテクノロジーから，人々にとって魅力的な場合に使用されるテクノロジーへ，③国家経済主体から

世界市場経済へ，④短期的観点から長期的観点へ，⑤中央集権化から地方分権化へ，⑥政府等の組織的支援から，自助へ，⑦代表制民主主義から参加型民主主義へ，⑧階層からネットワーキングへ，⑨北東のバイアスから南西のバイアスへ，⑩物事を「二者択一」でとらえることから，複数の選択肢をもつことへ。

30年後，Naisbittの予測は正しいことが証明された。

この変化とは何か。産業革命以来，最大の変化だろうか。筆者は史上最大といえるほどの変化だと確信している。この変化は無限に続き，無限に広がる。Arthur（2011）はセカンド・エコノミー（第二の経済）という概念を提示している。ワットの蒸気機関が登場した1760年代あたりから1850年頃にかけての産業革命の到来により，経済は機械の力という形で筋肉系を発展させた。そして現在は神経系を発展させつつある。1990年頃にはコンピュータ同士の通信が始まり，あらゆる場所でこうした接続が開始された。個々のマシン（サーバー）はいわばニューロンであり，軸索とシナプスは相互に接続して適切な行動を取れるようにするコミュニケーションの経路とリンケージである。

20世紀初頭，農場の仕事は機械化され，農業労働の必要性は低下した。その数十年後には，製造の仕事が機械化され，工場労働の必要性も低下した。現在，サービス部門の多くのビジネスプロセスが機械化されつつあり，必要とされる人員が減少することで体系的な雇用削減という圧力が生じている。

ところで，ここから得られる教訓は何だろうか。

21世紀の主要な成長原動力のひとつとして，セカンド・エコノミーは多くの雇用機会を生み出すことなく繁栄を生み出している。今日の社会は，繁栄を生み出す代わりにいかにして分配するかという大きな課題に直面している。従来の共通認識のとおり，富は仕事と関連しているべきである。農業の仕事が段階的に縮小した時点で，世の中には製造の仕事が創出された。さらに，ブルーカラーの製造業が縮小し，ホワイトカラーのサービス業が拡大した。そしてデジタル社会への移行によって，こうしたサービス業も縮小しつつある。将来的にホワイトカラーのビジネスプロセスを伴う雇用は減少すると考えられるため，私たちは問題に直面しているのである。

第 4 章　栄光と夢

　筆者は，過去 30 年間に，他の先進工業国が「筋肉系」の構築から「神経系」の開発へと変化している間に，日本で何が生じていたかを探ってきた。その筋肉系を構築する上で，日本は製造業においてトヨタに代表される多くの一流ブランドを世界的な有力企業として確立させた。アメリカ人でさえも，技術とイノベーションだけでなく，そのマネジメントシステムまでトヨタから学んでいる。しかし，今後も日本がこれまでのように強さを保てるかという点については疑問が残る。日本は情報通信技術（ICT）の牽引役であった。日本がアメリカの「アップル」に対抗するためには，韓国におけるサムスンのように，自国の「アップル」を生み出す必要が生じている。最近，ソニーとパナソニックの信用格付けが投機的水準にまで引き下げられたことからも，イノベーションにおける日本の指導的立場が急速に悪化していることがわかる。

4.3　新しい潮流

　次に，私たちの博物館部門に生じたことを検討しよう。

　1990 年から 2000 年にかけて，200 館の博物館が中央政府，地方自治体，およびコミュニティによって設立された。日本は，博物館発展の絶頂期にあって，博物館のビジョンとミッション管理を見失った。こうした博物館の病的状況を経て，日本の博物館団体は改革のために成すべきことを認識するに至った。「メセナ」（企業による芸術活動の支援）によって，博物館および芸術振興のための支援，奨励，促進，または財政援助に向けた官民パートナーシップ（PPP）が導入された。一般市民は，21 世紀に備えるための生涯学習を意識し始めた。2000 年から，日本ミュージアム・マネジメント学会（JMMA）は博物館評価のための格付けシステムを開発した。バランススコアカード（BSC）等の各種方法論を用いてパフォーマンス管理が導入されたほか，市民参加型社会教育に向けたデジタル化，対話，そしてコミュニケーションが提唱された。2002 年の教育改革により，高校生の社会教育の一環として総合学習の時間が設けられた。

　とはいえ，官民による博物館部門への資金援助および支援は，十分というに

は程遠い。個人的には，19世紀末までに日本の中央政府が行ったことを今日再び適用できるのではないかと考える。文化的資源のプランニングと管理における国家的イニシアチブは，将来のナショナル・イノベーションに沿った博物館の社会的使命と公共サービスをもたらすことができるだろう。

オーストラリア政府は，文化の発展とイノベーションの重要性を認識した。Cutler（2008）は，イノベーションに関する研究を通じて，文化および芸術を経済発展と明確に結びつけた。そしてイノベーション・産業・科学・研究省に対する報告書「冒険するオーストラリア：イノベーションにおける力の構築」の中で，文化と芸術の自己認識と公的なイノベーションの枠組みや政策，プログラムとの間に大きな隔たりがあったことを指摘した。202ページにわたるこの報告書は，他の先進国を研究しただけでなく，中国やインドなどの新興国にも注目した。Cutlerは，イノベーションが21世紀の重要な原動力のひとつであると確信し，「すべてのオーストラリア人の中にイノベーション精神を育むべきである」[1]と指摘した。

4.4　結語

人々の働き方やライフスタイルは，デジタル化によって劇的に変化した。中国やインドのような第三世界の国に旅行する際，スマートフォンが青物市の露天商に至るまで広く普及している様子を見ても驚くことはないだろう。アフリカと中東のジャスミン革命は，インターネットが民主主義の発展に与える影響を示すもうひとつの例である。Nielson（2009）の報告書によると，世界のインターネット人口の3分の2がソーシャルネットワークやブログサイトを訪問しており，こうした部門は今やインターネット使用時間のほぼ10％を占めている。

2007年にウィーンで採択されたICOM規約は，博物館を「社会とその発展に貢献し，教育，研究，娯楽のために人間とその環境の有形，無形の文化遺産を収集，保存，調査研究，伝達，展示を行う公衆に開かれた非営利の常設機関である」[2]と定義している。

第 4 章　栄光と夢

　現在のクラウドコンピューティングやソーシャルメディアの発展を踏まえて，筆者は第 6 世代の博物館の時代が到来したと考えている。第 6 世代の博物館とは，文化資源の統合と管理のための卓越した中心的存在である。日本は先進国として，他のアジア諸国と協力し 21 世紀における地域文化の復興と繁栄のために社会的責任を果たすことができるであろうと筆者は確信している。産業の時代にあって，日本はトヨタに代表される強力な「筋肉系」を構築した。これからは，情報社会へと移行する中で，ソニーやパナソニックを通じた過去の栄光を再構築し，強力な「神経系」を獲得することだろう。それは，私たちアジア太平洋地域の博物館と博物館の専門家の使命であろう。

注・引用文献
 1：Cutler (2008). Report: Venturous Australia – Building Strength in Innovation, Sydney, Ministry for Innovation, Industry, Science and Research.
 2：ICOM Statutes, Approved in Vienna (Austria) August 24, 2007, p.2. <http://icom.museum/fileadmin/user_upload/pdf/Statuts/statutes_eng.pdf>

参考文献
Arthur (2011). "The Second Economy," McKinsey Quarterly, <http://www.mckinsey-quarterly.com/The_second_economy_2853#AboutTheAuthor>
CIA (2011). The World Factbook <https://www.cia.gov/library/publications/the-world-factbook/>
Cutler (2008). Report: Venturous Australia – Building Strength in Innovation, Sydney, Ministry for Innovation, Industry, Science and Research.
Dippel (2002). The Language of Conscience, Brenham, Texas, Texas Peacemaker Publications, LLC.
Naisbitt (1982). Mega Trends: Ten New Directions Transform Our Lives, New York, NY, U.S.A., Grand Central Publishing.
Nielson (2009). "Global Faces and Network Places: A Nelson Report on Social Networking's New Global Footprints," Nielson Company.
Wang (2011). "Challenges & Opportunities in Museum Development A Historic-Sociological Perspective: China versus Japan," Proceeding of ICOM CECA Zagreb, Croatia.

Wang, W. (2006). "Scientific Outlook: Concept and Practice," Beijing, Central Party School Press.

World Bank (2011). World Development Indicators database <http://siteresources.worldbank.org/DATASTATISTICS/Resources/GDP.pdf>

第**5**章

博物館，図書館，アーカイブズを変容させる触媒としてのデジタルエンゲージメント
フィールド自然史博物館の事例研究

5.1 背景

Wang（2012）は，ソーシャルメディアとデジタル化が博物館に与える影響を検討した。こうした変化とは何か。産業革命以来の最大の変化だろうか。筆者は史上最大といえるほどの変化だと確信している。この変化は無限に続き，無限に広がる。博物館，図書館，アーカイブズ（以下，「MLA」）が，利用者に対する見方を変えつつあるというだけではない。利用者側もMLAに対する見方を変えつつあるのである。MLAの役割は内外から再考されており，その結果としてMLAに期待されるものも大きく変化している。芸術，歴史，文化を専門的に取り扱うという役割は残っているが，その社会的機能は従来のそれとは異なってきている。

Dippel（2002）は，社会発展の主な推進要因として政治，経済，知識，メディアを挙げている。数名の著名な社会学者は早くも1970年から，時代は将来的に古い産業社会から新しい情報社会へと移行する傾向があると述べていた。今日，ソーシャルメディア，デジタルモビリティ，そしてクラウドコンピューティングが人々の考え方や働き方を変えつつある。

Toffler（1980）は，文化と地域社会の発展を表す「第三の波」理論を生み出した。第一の波は，それまでの狩猟採集民の文化を覆した新石器革命以来，世界の大部分で広く普及した定住農業社会である。第二の波は産業化時代の社会であり，産業革命によって西ヨーロッパで始まり，次いで世界中に広がった。第三の波は，脱産業社会である。Tofflerは，1950年代後半以降，ほとんどの

国が第二の波の社会から第三の波の社会に移行しつつあると述べている。彼はそれを記述するために多くの言葉を作り出し，「情報化時代」といった他人が発明した造語にも言及している。

　筆者は本稿で，デジタルエンゲージメントがMLAの将来的な発展と現在の運営に与える影響を明らかにしつつ，新たな現象を検討する。そのためには，MLAの戦略的マネジメントの横断的研究が必要となる。基準となる情報を得るために，シカゴのMLAによる，地域の教育，文化，経済システムに対する総合的アプローチを検討する。具体的には，フィールド博物館が2006年から2015年にかけて行った，イノベーションを通じた発展を縦断的に研究する。

5.2　MLAにとっての課題と好機

　1976年から1979年にかけて，全米6都市を巡回した「ツタンカーメンの秘宝」展は，古代エジプトのファラオの墓から出土した見ごたえのある遺物を特集し，何百万人もの人々が博物館に詰めかけた。ツタンカーメンを一目見ようと数時間に及ぶ行列ができ，博物館の展示は「大ヒット」という新たな展開を記録したのである。10年以上前，MLAの幹部たちは，大規模な展覧会から重点を移し，地域社会への関与を優先事項とした。展示を巡回させる費用は法外に高額である。1980年代であればおそらく可能であっただろう全国巡回展は，現在では実現不可能である。

　21世紀には，MLAへの来館者はそれぞれの期待をもって施設を訪れるだろう。そして自らバーチャル展示をキュレートしたり，ソーシャルメディアを通じて収蔵品に関する情報を共有したり，関心のある問題に関する公開討論に参加したりすることで，展示コンテンツとふれあうだろう。MLAはまた，周囲の多様なコミュニティを反映する新旧の利用者にアピールするためには，展示室の壁を壊すことが必要だと認識しつつある。

第 5 章 博物館，図書館，アーカイブズを変容させる触媒としてのデジタルエンゲージメント

5.3 フィールド自然史博物館を研究対象とした理由

　シカゴのフィールド自然史博物館は，世界最大の自然史博物館のひとつであり，その教育・科学プログラムの規模と質によって，最高の自然史博物館としての地位を維持している。フィールド博物館自体は，8万平方メートルの建物スペースを占有する MLA が一体となった施設であり，その収集センターには 2,470 万点の標本があり，毎年 20 万点が追加されている。図書館には書籍 27 万 5,000 冊，国内外の新聞雑誌 278 誌，記録資料 1,800 フィート，希少本 7,500 冊，芸術作品 3,000 点が所蔵されている。写真アーカイブは 30 万枚に上る。同博物館には 800〜900 名の客員教授と研究者がおり，毎年世界中から 200 万人が訪れる。

　フィールド博物館は，アメリカのほとんどの博物館と同じく，主に民間の資金に支えられている非営利団体である。明確に定義されたガバナンス体制（地域社会の代表を含む理事会）で，記録管理も非常に優れており，博物館が誕生した 1983 年の初日から今日に至るまでの年次報告書が入手できる。

　周知のとおり，博物館で展示できるのは収蔵品の 1％以下である。フィールド博物館は，収蔵品をより広く公開するためのインターネットのインフラを整備する目的で，情報技術プラットフォームのアップグレードに多大な資金を投入した。その具体例は以下のとおりである。同博物館は，10 年にわたる努力を通じて，公式ウェブサイトを知識の源に変換し，早くも 2007 年から，世界中で 900 万人以上のサイト訪問者に素晴らしいリソースを提供している。同サイトは 2 万 7,500 ページを超えるもので，指導者用の詳細なガイドから，フィールドサイエンティストに向けたダウンロード可能な参考資料まで，幅広い内容が揃っている。2010 年，フィールド博物館の科学者たちは，シカゴのオースティン地区の学生とフィジーの学生とをつなぐプロジェクトを指揮した。これにより，シカゴの学生は，太平洋のサンゴ礁環境を体験し，科学的プロセスに関与し，現実世界の保護に参加することができた。プロジェクト参加者は，800 人以上の応募を集めた「2010 Digital Media and Learning Competition

Award（デジタルメディア・学習コンクール賞）」と題する助成金コンペ受賞者の小グループで構成されていた[1]。

　フィールド博物館はその後も，訪問者を引きつけるための先進技術の導入に財源を割り当て続けた。2014 年には，インターネットサービスを 1Gbps（ギガビット／秒）のイーサネット専用インターネット接続にアップグレードし，予約帯域幅は 10Gbps となった。新たな IT インフラで確保した帯域幅によって，訪問者がコレクション，コンテンツ，展示品を探求し，これに関与するためのニーズを満たす対話型技術がサポートされ，また博物館のオペレーションが強化された（Segal, 2014）。

　インターネットセレブリティから博物館の科学者へ。Emily Graslie の事例は，フィールド博物館がコミュニケーションの新形態を取り入れていることを如実に物語る。Emily はスタジオアートを専攻する 20 歳の大学生だった時，ふと思いついてフィールド博物館を訪問した。そして 4 年後，同館の「Chief Curiosity Correspondent（好奇心の通信局長）」に就任し，20 万人以上の登録者をもつ教育的な YouTube チャンネルである Brain Scoop で司会者を務めている。
　来館者がオリジナルを損なうことなく収蔵品と触れ合えるよう，同館は最新の 3D 印刷技術を取り入れて歴史的遺物の複製を作成した。その一例が，「ミイラ：墓所からの新しい秘密」と題した全米巡回展である。ミイラの「中をのぞく」ために医療用 CT スキャナを使用。来館者は，脆い標本の横に置かれた大型卓上コンピュータのスキャンを操作して，墓所から出土した覆いの下の衣服，髪型，宝石をのぞき見することができる。

5.3.1　フィールド博物館のミッション・ステートメント

　フィールド博物館は，自然界や文化の多様性と関係性に関わる教育機関である。人類学，植物学，地質学，古生物学，動物学の分野を組み合わせ，学際的アプローチを採用して，地球物理，植物，動物，人間，そして文化

第 5 章　博物館，図書館，アーカイブズを変容させる触媒としてのデジタルエンゲージメント

の過去，現在，未来に関する知識を向上させる[2]。

5.3.2　フィールド博物館の経済的影響に関するステートメント

以下はフィールド博物館の 2011 年の運営状況の抜粋である[3]。

- 60 回以上の調査旅行を行い，200 種の新しい動植物を発見
- アマゾン川上流で 110 万エーカー以上の熱帯雨林を保護
- アメリカ全州および世界 40 カ国以上から 128 万人の来館者
- 1,000 件の科学教育プログラムに，35 万 4,000 人以上の大人と子どもが参加
- 780 人の客員研究員，53 人の研究生，164 人のインターンを受け入れ

図 1 は，同館の収集をベースとした研究と学習が地域社会に与えた経済的影響，および公衆の現代世界に対する理解と評価の向上に与えた影響を示している。

5.4　デジタルエンゲージメントの活用

5.4.1　デジタルエンゲージメントの活用による社会発展の促進

2012 年，グレインジャー財団はフィールド博物館に対し，デジタルエンゲージメントの大きな飛躍を支援するために特別な贈り物をした。この助成金の目的は，技術インフラ，収蔵品のデジタル画像化，新たなデジタル学習ラボ計画，展示用のデジタル技術，および利用者への新たなオファーの開発という 5 つのイニシアチブを調査検討することでであった。この検討には，科学研究のための CT スキャナから，建物の Wi-Fi システムの改善に至るデジタルエンゲージメントも含まれた。

Slover Linett Audience Research Inc.（2014）は，上記の調査検討を 2 年間，2 段階に分けて行った。第 1 段階の主目的は，博物館の来館者が潜在的に秘めている可能性のある，動機，好み，経験を明らかにすることである（Slover

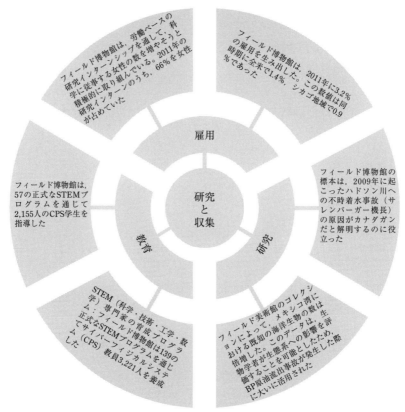

図1 2011年 フィールド博物館が与えた経済的影響
出典：The Field Museum's Impact to Local Community[4] を改変

Linett Audience Research Inc., 2013a）。そして第2段階の主目的は以下のとおりである。

予備的な第1段階で明らかにされた，動機，意味づけの優先順位，およびテクノロジーに対する理想の普及状況を定量化し測定すること。

これらの動機と理想に基づいて来館者という母体の中に存在する傾向別のセグメントを特定すること。その目的は，さまざまに異なる来館者のニーズに最適な形で対応できるよう，博物館が新たなテクノロジーを取り入れる戦略を定める助けとすることにある（Slover Linett Audience Research Inc., 2013b）。

第 5 章　博物館，図書館，アーカイブズを変容させる触媒としてのデジタルエンゲージメント

　博物館の体験への来館者の期待に応えるために，どのようにテクノロジーを活用できるだろうか。上記の検討の結果，2つの道筋が提案されている。すなわち，テクノロジーを活用して博物館コンテンツ（自然および人類文化）によりいっそう近づく方法を生み出すこと。そして来館者たちと経験や意味づけを共有するためのプラットフォームを生み出すことである。

5.4.2　セグメント別に異なる来館者の期待

　定量的な調査によって，来館者の大半は館内で新しいデジタルツールを見ると興奮することが確認された。来館者の約 4 分の 3 は，新技術が来館体験をさらに良いものにする可能性があると考えており，3 分の 2 は博物館がこうした技術を「ぜひ」いっそう展示に組み込んでほしいと述べた。実際，テクノロジーに対する関心のレベルは，年齢，教育，所得といった人口統計学的要因にほとんど無関係だった。新技術に興奮する来館者の数は高齢層も若年層もほぼ同じであり，博物館をハイテク装置からはるか遠いオアシスととらえている若者が，高齢者とほぼ同じくらい存在することが明らかとなった。

　調査で明らかとなったもうひとつの重要なポイントは，多くの来館者が，博物館体験の記憶をとどめるため，自分のテクノロジーを既に館内で使用しているという点である。それも非常にソーシャルな，時にはユーモラスな方法で（来館者の約 4 分の 3 が館内でカメラやスマートフォン，タブレットを使って写真撮影すると答えている）。これより数は少ないものの，来館中に興味を抱いた質問やテーマを調べる（23 %），または帰宅後にそうした情報を調べる（38 %）など，展示体験をさらに高めるものとして自分のデバイスを使用する人々もいる。

　フィールド博物館は，セグメント別に異なる博物館体験のニーズをカバーするために，どの展覧会においても，より伝統的な展示方法と幅広いデジタル体験・テクノロジー体験を戦略的に組み合わせる「多層的」アプローチを開発した。こうした組み合わせの比率は，展覧会の目標，対象とする観客，そして場合によっては博物館全体における体験の順序や配置の意図によって異なる。表 1

表1 動機，関与の方法，テクノロジーの好み別に分類した来館者の類型学

セグメント	好奇心旺盛な活動探究者	瞑想的な伝統主義者	社交的な探検者	親－ファシリテーター
来館者の期待	32 %	24 %	18 %	16 %
フィールド博物館の経験から得たいもの	知的成長，新たな知識や視点の獲得，シカゴ有数の名所を体験（主に観光客）	関心のある特定のテーマ（特に自然）への関与，新たな知識や視点の獲得	愛する人と関係をもつ，リラックスと再充電	子どもたちに豊かで教育的な体験を提供する
博物館のコンテンツにどのように関与するのが好きか	対話的，直接手で触れる，個別に楽しめる参加体験	人工遺物を見て解釈する，同行者と語る	同行者と語る，アイデアや展示内容の自由な探求	対話的，直接手で触れる，子どもと一緒に楽しめる参加型の体験
期待する博物館体験に役立つテクノロジー	博物館の「ベストオブ」を見るためのモバイルアプリツアー。想定を覆す新しい視点をもたらすことを重視した，対話型デジタル技術	博物館体験に干渉しないこと。自然や人類文化と親しく語り合う場である展覧会では，主に手持ちまたは邪魔にならない技術の使用を検討する	意味づけや記憶形成を共有するプラットフォームとして役立つ，コンテンツやゲームなどを自由に探検できる対話型ディスプレイ	ゲームやミニ「科学実験」ができるデジタルディスプレイ。その他の対話型活動。同時に，より伝統的な体験活動

出 典：Slover Linett Audience Research Inc. (2014). What Makes a Great Museum Experience and How Can Technology Help? Visitor Research and Segmentation for The Field Museum's Grainger Initiatives, p. 9[5]。

はこのプロセスに関して良い参考となる。

　すべての展示企画スタッフは，これらの主要4セグメントのニーズを少なくとも考慮する必要があるが，だからといってすべての展示会において各セグメントを等しく関与させようと試みる必要があるわけではない。展示スタッフは，さまざまに異なる観客のニーズに合わせて，展示体験の様相を調節することができる。観客に関する知識に照らして，意図的かつ戦略的な決定を下すことが重要である。

第 5 章　博物館，図書館，アーカイブズを変容させる触媒としてのデジタルエンゲージメント

5.5　MLA の社会的使命

Wang（2009）によると，MLA を良知，知恵，芸術の展示を通して文明を解釈する知識の源と見なすことは，世界的に新たな傾向となっている。2007 年にウィーンで採択された ICOM 規約は，博物館を「社会とその発展に貢献し，教育，研究，娯楽のために人間とその環境の有形，無形の文化遺産を収集，保存，調査研究，伝達，展示を行う公衆に開かれた非営利の常設機関である」[6] と定義している。

ICOM 規約は当初，「収蔵」に重点を置いて作成されたが，ほどなく 1951 年には「保存，研究，向上」を含むよう修正された。2007 年には「研究と楽しみ」を超えて「教育」が博物館の基本的業務における最優先の共通目的とされた。ICOM のコミュニティが博物館の公共サービスに特別な注意を払ったことは，その社会的使命への重点的な取り組みを反映するものだった。また，地域特有の文化や遺産，基本的価値を一般に浸透させるために博物館部門が果たした役割の重要性も反映していた。

5.6　博物館の戦略的位置づけの認識

21 世紀，人々は生活を楽しむための余暇の時間をより長くとるようになり，専門的能力を発展させるための生涯学習プログラムに参加している。博物館が，利用者の発展と来館者へのサービス向上を重視するようになるにつれ，潜在的な利用者に対して与えられるレジャーや学習の機会の選択肢を提供する情報は，量においてもチャンネルにおいてもますます膨大なものとなっている。そのため，人々の間では時間をレジャーに使うか学習に使うかという競合が生じている。したがって，公衆による博物館への関与を拡大するにあたっては，競争の激化という課題が生じている。博物館の幹部たちにとって，優先順位の高い利用者に対して博物館がいっそう効果的にアプローチできるよう，ポジショニングやブランディング戦略の活用方法を特定することがますます重要と

なっている。博物館は，その社会的使命に基づいて自らの責任を果たすために，自らが提供するものを有意義かつ記憶に残る文脈の中に位置づける必要がある。

　Prevenost（2013）は，American Association of Community Theater（アメリカコミュニティシアター協会）の依頼を受けて，文化産業がブランディング，ポジショニング，戦略的課題に対する理解を深めるための調査を行った。アイデンティティのブランディングとは，自分が何者であるかを問題とし，組織のポジショニングとは，自分の位置づけを問題とし，戦略的なポジショニングとは，他者との間に望む位置取りを問題とする。博物館の幹部たちは，博物館の目標と地域社会の発展の目標とをいかに一致させることができるかを理解する必要がある。そして，他の組織との関連でどのように認識されたいのかを理解し，その結論を，プログラム開発，寄付者へのサービス，施設計画，年間イベントスケジュールから特別なイベントに至るまで，全体的に適用する必要がある。効果的なポジショニングによって，あらゆる博物館は，自らの強みを活用し，コミュニケーションの方向性を定め，資金調達，開発，および組織改善の努力を支える論拠を補強できるだろう。

　事例研究で取り上げた博物館のミッション・ビジョンステートメントを以下に挙げる。主要な博物館が自らをどのように位置づけようとしているかが明らかである。

シカゴ美術館
シカゴ美術館は，公衆に創造的刺激を与え教育することを目的に，業界最高の倫理基準および実践に従い，世界の多様な芸術的伝統を象徴する，最高品質の芸術作品を収集，保存，解釈する。

シカゴ科学産業博物館
当博物館の使命は，すべての人の創造的な才能を刺激することである。当博物館のビジョンは，子どもたちが科学，技術，医学，工学における潜在能力を最大限に発揮できるよう鼓舞し，動機づけることである。

Kotler（2008）は，ポジショニングを「競合相手との関係においてその組織が意味するものを消費者が理解し，評価し，魅力を感じるように，組織のイメージ，価値，提供物を設計する行為」[7]と定義している。

Mosena（2011）は，2010年の年次報告書で次のように述べている。「6年間の入念な計画，素晴らしいサポート，そして確実な実施によって，シカゴ科学産業博物館（MSI）は Science Rediscovered capital campaign（科学再発見資金キャンペーン）の任務を遂に完了した。合計で2億880万ドルの資金が集まった。厳しい経済状況下にあって，これは大きな成果といえる。当博物館は現在，21世紀型の科学教育とプログラム作成の新しいモデルとなっている。そして，子どもたちが科学，技術，医学，工学の分野で最大限に潜在力を発揮できるよう，鼓舞し，動機づけするというビジョンを追求する上で，非常に良いポジショニングにある」[8]。2004年から2010年にかけて，経済環境がかなり厳しかったにもかかわらず，ひとつの博物館が2億880万ドルの資金を集めたという事実は，適切な戦略計画が整えば地域社会が博物館を支援する可能性があるということを明確に裏づけた。

次に，地域社会への影響を見てみよう。シカゴの World Business Report（2011）によると，2011年には景気は引き続き回復の兆しを見せている。教育，医療，専門／ビジネスサービスで雇用が回復し，シカゴ地域の生産高は3.2％増加した。輸出は前年比2％増であった（化学および産業機械の輸出はそれぞれ25％以上増）。シカゴ地域の商業地区と開発拠点の売上高は，2011年に83％増加した（2010年の59億ドルに対して108億ドル）。その筆頭となったのは工業出荷であり，2010年の8億ドルから2011年には28億ドルに改善した。全米ベンチャーキャピタル協会によると，2011年はシカゴ地域のスタートアップ企業にとって特に活動が活発な年であり，2001年以降，最高額のベンチャーキャピタルが調達された。シカゴ市が受賞した賞，これは，博物館が自らの使命を地域社会と合わせることに関して大きな進歩を遂げつつあるという実例である。

5.7 ソーシャルメディアは水路か洪水か

　Richardson（2011）は，ソーシャルメディアのトップ3であるFacebook，Twitter，Kloutからデータを入手する方法を生み出し，3,635館の博物館や美術館を追跡した結果，Facebook上では1,186万3,882人の「いいね」を，Twitter上では1,290万9,649人の「フォロワー」を発見した。各博物館には平均8,000人のフォロワーがおり，ボランティアとして私たちの日常業務に注意を払い，自分の意見を表明するだけでなく，投票によって私たちの仕事を評価している。水は航行のための水路を作り出すが，一方で船を沈めさせることもある。博物館の専門家は，Facebook，Twitter，YouTubeなどのソーシャルメディアの幅広い活用に特別な注意を払う必要がある。

　Wang（2012）は，ソーシャルメディアの強い影響を受けて，将来の博物館が変化してゆく上でプロセスオーナーシップが及ぼす影響について懸念を表明した。従来の博物館学芸員は，変化と発展のために尽力してきた。だがもはや時代は変わった。今日，ソーシャルメディアは，物理的博物館およびデジタル博物館で人々が見たいものに影響を与えるだけでなく，一般の人々が情報を入手する方法やその情報を知識へと変える方法にまで影響を与える可能性がある。図2は，MLA研究におけるプロセスオーナーシップの全体像を示している。興味深いことに，情報フローはビジネスにおけるプロセスオーナーシップの各層とはかなりかけ離れている。

　デジタル化は人々の働き方やライフスタイルを変えた。Neilson（2009）の報告によると，世界のインターネット人口の3分の2がソーシャルネットワークやブログサイトを訪問しており，現在この部門がインターネット使用時間のほぼ10％を占めている。Dicker（2009）は，オーストラリア，イギリス，アメリカ，ノルウェー，ニュージーランドの計96人の学芸員に対して「学芸員の生活にブログその他のソーシャルメディアが及ぼす影響」と題する調査を行った。その結果，博物館学芸員の役割がソーシャルメディアによって大きく影響を受けていることが明らかとなった。ソーシャルメディアは新たな意見や

新たな票決方法を生み出し，サイバー空間における拡張展示の管理に新しい次元を加える可能性がある。

技術開発は博物館に新たなプラットフォームを誕生させた。これは博物館の学芸員にどのような影響を与えるだろうか。学芸員はソーシャルメディアをキュレーションの実践に取り入れているだろうか。取り入れている場合，ソーシャルメディアの空間でどのように交流しているのだろうか。そしてこれらすべてが学芸員の役割と彼らが手がける収集コレクションにどのような影響を与えているのだろうか。フィールド博物館は，階層を隔てる壁を取り払うことで，情報フローに関して最善の事業プロセスを生み出した。デジタルエンゲージメントが，MLAを社会発展のための知識の源に変える触媒であることが証明された形である。

図3は，すべての「壁」が撤廃された様子を示している。たとえば，フィールド博物館の展覧会「ミイラ：墓所からの新しい秘密」では，CTスキャナの使用によって，物理的展示とデジタル展示との間にあった明確な境界が取り払われた。

図2　ソーシャルメディアの影響　　　図3　地域社会文化のリソースの統合

5.8 教訓

　フィールド博物館と同様の事例は他にもある。こうした現象は，アメリカの政治的，経済的，文化的な土壌に根ざしている。アメリカには12万3,000館の図書館と1万7,500館の博物館が存在する。連邦政府機関である博物館・図書館サービス機構（IMLS）は，図書館や博物館が，助成金，研究，政策展開，および国家的パートナーシップを通じて，イノベーション，生涯学習，そして市民の文化活動への参加を促進するよう奨励している。

　シカゴ市には，100館以上の博物館，美術館，その他の文化機関，および80拠点に及ぶ中央図書館がある[9]。シカゴの国立公文書館には，52万7,000点の人工遺物を記述した，国家記録の81％を占める約100億の論理データ記録が存在する。すでにデジタル化された資料のデジタルコピーも92万2,000件ある[10]。IMLSの報告書は「（中略）私たちが最優先すべき目標をいかに達成したかについて，多くの実例を提示する。その目標とは，博物館や図書館による魅力的な学習体験の提供を支援すること，博物館や図書館を強力なコミュニティアンカーとすること，博物館や図書館のコレクション管理を支援すること，およびコンテンツへのアクセスを増すためのテクノロジーの活用を推進することである」[11]。

　フィールド博物館，科学産業博物館，シカゴ美術館，シカゴ中央図書館，およびシカゴ国立公文書館は世界的な機関であり，MLA部門における革新と変化をリードしている。地域開発に向けて明確に定義されたその社会的使命を果たすためには，より包括的な官民パートナーシップ（PPP）モデルが不可欠である。

第 5 章　博物館，図書館，アーカイブズを変容させる触媒としてのデジタルエンゲージメント

注・引用文献
1：フィールドミュージアムのウェブサイトおよび過去 10 年間の年次報告書の要約です。
https://www.fieldmuseum.org/about/history
https://www.fieldmuseum.org/about/annual-reports
2：Office of Academic Affairs（1997）. THE FIELD MUSEUM COLLECTIONS AND RESEARCH FEBRUARY 1997, p. 4. <https://www.fieldmuseum.org/sites/default/files/annual_report1997_0.pdf>
3：The Field Museum Annual Report 2011, p. 1. <https://www.fieldmuseum.org/sites/default/files/2011 Annual Report 0.pdf>
4：The Field Museum's Impact to Local Community <https://www.fieldmuseum.org/sites/default/files/Economic%20Impact%20State ment%20 2011-modified.pdf>
5：Slover Linett Audience Research Inc.（2014）. What Makes a Great Museum Experience and How Can Technology Help? Visitor Research and Segmentation for The Field Museum's Grainger Initiatives, p. 9. <http://www.slaudienceresearch.com/files/publications/Executive%20summary%20-%20Field%20Museum%20visitor%20experience%20and%20technology%20research%20-%2 0Slover%20Linett.pdf>
6：ICOM Statutes, Approved in Vienna（Austria）August 24, 2007, p. 2. <http://icom.museum/fileadmin/user_upload/pdf/Statuts/statutes_eng.pdf>
7：Kotler P.（2008）*Museum Marketing and Strategy: Designing Missions, Building Audiences, Generating Revenue and Resources,* John Wiley & Sons, San Francisco, p. 130.
8：Mosena（2011）. Annual Report of Museum of Science and Technology, Chicago <http://www.msichicago.org/join-and-support/leadership/annual-report/>
9：Chicago Central Library <https://en.wikipedia.org/wiki/Chicago Public Library>
10：National Archives at Chicago <https://www.archives.gov/chicago>
11：IMLS 2013 Annual Report, p. 1. <https://www.imls.gov/publications/2013-annual-report>

* IMLS Institute of Museum and Library Services is a federal government agency in the U.S. The agency is funded through the U.S. Congress.

参考文献
Chicago Central Library <https://en.wikipedia.org/wiki/Chicago Public Library>
Chicago World Business Report 2011 <https://www.dropbox.com/s/4qrpwddycjdtkw8/WBC-2011-Annual-Report.pdf?dl=0>

Dicker (2009). "The Impact of Blogs and Other Social Media on the Life of a Curator", <http://www.museumsandtheweb.com/mw2010/papers/dicker/dicker.html#ixzz29dRORoy N>

Dippel (2002). The Language of Conscience, Brenham, Texas, Texas Peacemaker Publications, LLC., pp. 22-102.

Field Museum technology project wins prestigious award <https://www.eurekalert.org/pub releases/2010-05/fm-fmt051010.php>

How Emily Graslie went from YouTube science star to full-time at the Field Museum <http://www.chicagoreader.com/chicago/field-museum-emily-graslie-brainscoop-youtube/Content?oid= 12236428>

IMLS 2013 Annual Report <https://www.imls.gov/publications/2013-annual-report>

Kotler P. (2008). *Principles of Marketing,* New York, Pearson Prentice Hall, pp. 281-348.

List of Museums and Cultural Institutes in Chicago <https://en.wikipedia.org/wiki/List of museums and cultural institutions in Chicago>

Mosena (2011). Annual Report of Museum of Science and Technology, Chicago <http://www.msichicago.org/join-and-support/leadership/annual-report/>

Museum Visitor Typology with Motivations, Engagement, and Technology Preferences <http://www.slaudienceresearch.com/files/publications/Executive%20summary%20-%20Field%20Museum%20visitor%20experience%20and%20technology%20research%20-%20Slover%20Linett.pdf>

National Archives at Chicago <https://www.archives.gov/chicago>

Nielson (2009). "Global Faces and Network Places: A Nielson Report on Social Networking's New Global Footprints," Nielson Company.

Prevenost (2013). Beyond Branding: Strategic Market Positioning, ARTS INSIGHTS – MARCH 2013.

Richardson (2011). "The Top 50 – Museums in Social Media" <http://litot.es/museums-in-social-media>

Segal, Jack (2014). "The Field Museum in Chicago Uses Advanced Technologies to Engage Visitors," Market Wired <http://www.marketwired.com/press-release/the-field-museum-in-chicagouses-advanced-technologies-to-engage-visitors-nasdaq-cmcsa-1899383.htm>

Slover Linett Audience Research Inc. (2013a). Field Museum・Grainger Initiatives, May 17, 2013, Phase 1: Exploratory Qualitative Research Report of Key Findings and Recommendations <http://www.slaudienceresearch.com/files/publications/Phase%201%20qualitative%20report%20-%20Field%20Museum%20Grainger%20research%20-%20Slover%20Linett.pdf>

Slover Linett Audience Research Inc. (2013b). Field Museum・Grainger Initiatives December 12, 2013, Phase 2: Visitor Survey and Segmentation Report of Key Findings and Recommendations <http://www.slaudienceresearch.com/files/publications/Phase%202%20survey%20and%20segmentation%20report%20-%20Field%20Museum%20Grainger%20research%20-% 2 0Slover%20Linett.pdf>

Slover Linett Audience Research Inc. (2014). What Makes a Great Museum Experience and How Can Technology Help? Visitor Research and Segmentation for The Field Museum's Grainger Initiatives <http://www.slaudienceresearch.com/files/publications/Executive%20summary%20-%20Field%20Museum%20visitor%20experience%20and%20technology%20research%20-%2 0Slover%20Linett.pdf>

The Field Museum 2007 Annual Report <https://www.fieldmuseum.org/sites/default/files/2007 Annual Report.pdf>

The Field Museum Annual Report 2011 <https://www.fieldmuseum.org/sites/default/files/2011 Annual Report 0.pdf>

The Field Museum's Impact to Local Community <https://www.fieldmuseum.org/sites/default/files/Economic%20Impact%20State ment%20 2011-modified.pdf>

Toffler (1980). *The Third Wave,* New York, U.S.A., William Morrow and Company, pp. 32-112.

Wang L. (2012). Museum 2.0 – An Extended Exhibition in the Cyber Space by Social Media, Proceeding of ICOM CECA, Yerevan, Armenia.

Wang, L. (2009). "Building Conscience Driven Culture by Regional Heritage – Social Mission of Museums for the 21st Century," Proceeding of ICOM ASPAC TOKYO, 2009.

＊上記のウェブサイトは 2017 年 1 月 1 日〜3 月 31 日に検索したものである。

第6章

情報科学による市民のエンパワーメント
サイバー空間における博物館，図書館，アーカイブズ

6.1 セカンド・エコノミーと社会発展

　過去30年間，サイバー空間の広範な開発と革新によって，私たちのライフスタイル，働き方，そして思考方法は変化してきた。たとえばiPhoneやiPadなどの「スマートな」デバイスは，MLA（博物館，図書館，アーカイブズ）の場所を訪問する前，最中，および後における情報の検索と共有を容易にした。今日のグローバル・ビレッジにあって，MLAはインターネット上のソーシャルネットワークを通じ，文化，遺産，言語の枠を超えて人々の目にさらされている。Statista Portal（2017）によれば，ソーシャルメディアネットワークのトップ5には合計60億人のユーザーがいる。

　サイバー空間における非公式学習の動きは，公式の教育を新たな形に変えつつある。MLAの専門家は，展示デザインの基準，教育カリキュラムの開発，

表1　ソーシャルメディアネットワーク　トップ5

ソーシャルメディア	ユーザー（単位：百万人）
Facebook	1,968
WhatsApp	1,200
YouTube	1,000
FaceBook Messenger	1,000
WeChat	889

出典：Statista Portal（2017）[1]

情報技術の応用，人材開発，そして消費者保護戦略をより積極的に再検討するようになっている。

地域社会の発展を目的とする成人教育の歴史から，教訓を引き出すことができよう。効果的なケーススタディは，私たちが情報技術の波に対処する際の課題に取り組む助けとなるだろう。

情報科学を用いた市民のエンパワーメントにおけるベストプラクティスを追求するために，MLAの戦略的位置づけに関する研究が人気のツールとなりつつある。21世紀におけるMLAの社会的使命の位置づけるためには，情報化時代におけるMLAの戦略的開発に関する将来動向分析を検討する必要がある。

戦略的マネジメントのためには，伝統的なルールと新しいルールの双方に対処すべきである。Tapscott（2010）は，情報化時代においてはニューエコノミーが社会発展と同時に存在すると指摘した。今日，資本主義が自由市場制度の文脈のまま機能し続ける中，ゲームのルールは基本的に同じである。しかし，21世紀型資本主義の特徴によって，オールドエコノミーとはまったく異なるニューエコノミーが形成されている。Tapscottの有名な「ニューエコノミーが存在する6つの理由」[2]を以下に挙げる。

1. 富の創造のための新しいインフラ。ネットワーク，特にインターネットは，経済活動と進歩の基礎となりつつある。鉄道，道路，電力網，電話が垂直統合型ビジネスをサポートしてきたのとは異なり，ネットワークによる水平垂直型の統合が，コミュニティをまったく新しい生態系に変え続けると考えられる。
2. 新たなビジネスモデル。ニューエコノミー企業をインターネット技術に基づく企業や電子商取引を基盤とするドットコム企業としてとらえない。
3. 新たな価値の源。今日のナレッジベースの経済では，価値は脳の力によって生み出される。
4. 新たな富の所有。かつて産業資本主義の時代には，シルクハットの大物実業家が富の大部分を所有していた。今日では，アメリカ人の60%が金融市場に資産をもち，最大の株主は労働年金基金である。

5. 新たな教育モデルと機関。産業革命後の時代，生涯学習に対する要求がはるかに高まった。学生主体の，マイペース型でインタラクティブな学習法が普及するにつれて，教授法のモデルも変化しつつある。
6. 新たなガバナンス。クラウドコンピューティングとビッグデータは，政府機関の各部門をさらに細分化し，効率を高めるだろう。縦方向ではなく横方向のガバナンス構造は，管理的な政府をサービス指向の政府に変えるだろう。

Web 2.0 の人気は 2006 年の TIME 誌「パーソン・オブ・ザ・イヤー（今年の人）」で明らかになった。カバー・ストーリーでは，Lev Grossmann が次のように説明している。「これはかつて見たことのない規模のコミュニティとコラボレーションに関するストーリーだ。壮大な知識の目録である Wikipedia や無数のチャンネルを備えた人々のネットワーク YouTube，そしてインターネット上のメトロポリス MySpace に関するものだ。多くの人々が一握りの者に独占されていた力を奪取し，無償で互いに助け合っていること，そしてそれが世界を変えるだけでなく，世界が変わる方法まで変える，ということについてのストーリーだ」[3]。

6.2 博物館の社会的使命と公共サービスの再考

6.2.1 社会的使命

Wang（2009）によると，MLA を良知，知恵，芸術の展示を通して文明を解釈する知識の源と見なすことは，世界的に新たな傾向となっている。2007 年にウィーンで採択された ICOM 規約は，博物館を「社会とその発展に貢献し，教育，研究，娯楽のために人間とその環境の有形，無形の文化遺産を収集，保存，調査研究，伝達，展示を行う公衆に開かれた非営利の常設機関である」[4] と定義している。国際博物館会議アジア太平洋地域連盟（ICOM ASPAC）2009 のテーマは，「アジア太平洋地域における博物館の中核的な価値の再考と地域遺産」であり，ICOM 2010 大会のテーマは「博物館と社会的調和」であった。

6.2.2　博物館の公共サービスに関する世界各国の実践

　過去30年にわたり，多くの国々が博物館の社会的使命と公共サービスを国民の生涯学習の支援や革新的な国家プログラムを創出する分野に取り入れてきた。たとえば，日本にあるおよそ6,000館の博物館は，公民館，図書館とともに国民の生涯学習を支える三本柱の一翼を担っている。一方，アメリカには12万3,000館の図書館と1万7,500館の博物館があり，博物館・図書館サービス機構（IMLS）は，これらの機関が無数の生涯学習者たちに模範的な公共サービスを提供できるよう支援することを目的に活動している（IMLS, 2013）。MLAを生涯学習のプラットフォームとするために，私たちは人々の認識を変える手助けをする必要がある。MLAにおける最前線の教育者は「ナレッジブローカー（知識の仲介者）」となるべきであり，知識の創造，獲得，消化吸収，利用から普及まで，知識仲介のライフサイクルの各段階で公衆に提供されるべきである。

　現在，文化部門が発展していることは，MLAにとってより多くの機会と課題を生み出すだろう。時間の経過とともに，新しい事業部門が生まれる一方で廃れてゆく部門もある。情報通信技術（ICT）が21世紀における第四産業の創造を推進しており，現代は情報時代または知識時代と名づけられている。

　映画，出版，音楽，ドラマ，オペラ，およびメディア関連の業界は文化産業に分類されているが，MLA部門はどのように位置づけるべきだろうか。MLAによる大規模なデータ通信は，文化産業を推進するための重要な要素，またはMLAの中核事業ととらえることができる。

6.3　サイバー空間における課題

6.3.1　会員コミュニティ

　デジタル化は人々の働き方やライフスタイルを変えた。Neilsonの報告によると，世界のインターネット人口の3分の2がソーシャルネットワークやブログサイトを訪問しており，現在この部門がインターネット使用時間のほぼ

10％を占めている（NIELSEN, 2009）。

6.3.2　ソーシャルメディアが博物館学芸員の新たな役割の創出に及ぼす影響

　博物館や博物館の専門家は，サイバー空間時代にあって情報技術の波を乗りこなす準備ができているだろうか。Dicker が行った調査によって，博物館学芸員の役割がソーシャルメディアによって大きく影響を受けていることが明らかとなった。学芸員の「エキスパート」や「スペシャリスト」としての伝統的な役割は縮小している（DICKER, 2010）。

　「研究者」や「ナレッジブローカー」という位置づけは，今日の学芸員の現実を正しく反映するものではない。ソーシャルメディアは新たな意見や新たな票決方法を生み出し，サイバー空間における拡張展示の管理に新しい次元を追加する可能性がある。

　技術開発は博物館に新たなプラットフォームを生み出した。これは博物館の学芸員にどのような影響を与えるだろうか。学芸員はソーシャルメディアをキュレーションの実践に取り入れているだろうか。取り入れている場合，ソーシャルメディアの空間でどのように交流しているのだろうか。そしてこれらすべてが学芸員の役割と彼らが手がけるコレクションにどのような影響を与えているのだろうか。学芸員は，以前は公開講座やアウトリーチ活動，ウェブサイト編集などスタッフ業務の領域であった双方向または多方向コミュニケーションの需要が増加する中で，さまざまな課題に直面している。

6.3.3　博物館ウェブサイトの進化：Web 1.0 から 2.0 へ

　一般に Web 2.0 の主な特徴と考えられている点は以下 4 項目である。

1. 情報共有（1 対 1，1 対多，多対 1，多対多）
2. 相互運用性（多様なシステムと組織がシームレスに連携して動く能力）
3. ユーザーフレンドリーな設計（ユーザー中心の原理）
4. コラボレーション（共通の目標のために複数の関係者が共同作業）

博物館のウェブサイトは，サイバー空間への入り口と考えられるソーシャルメディアの急速な発展の影響を受けて進化してきた。ソーシャルメディアの黎明期は AOL 時代と呼ばれ，ウェブサイトは単なる情報源として使われていた。博物館のウェブサイトは情報を提供し，訪問計画をサポートするように設計されていた。

Facebook の時代となった現在，潜在的な来場者はソーシャルネットワークの投稿を通じて博物館を見つけることができる。ソーシャルメディアがウェブへの入り口となり，会員コミュニティの及ぼす強い影響力によって，博物館の専門家の役割は真剣に問い直されることとなろう。博物館学芸員がソーシャルネットワークを利用することは，管理上必要な役割だと見なされるべきである。

6.4　MLA の戦略的管理

6.4.1　MLA の戦略的位置づけの認識

21 世紀，人々は生活を楽しむための余暇の時間をより長くとるようになり，専門的能力を発展させるための生涯学習プログラムに参加している。MLA が，利用者の増加と来場者へのサービス向上を重視するようになるにつれ，潜在的な利用者に対して与えられるレジャーや学習の機会の選択肢を提供する情報は，量においてもチャンネルにおいてもますます膨大なものとなっている。そのため，公衆による MLA への関与を拡大するにあたっては，競争の激化という課題が生じている。

博物館の首脳陣にとって，MLA が優先順位の高い利用者に対していっそう効果的にアプローチできるよう，ポジショニングやブランディング戦略の活用方法を特定することがますます重要となっている。MLA は，その社会的使命に基づいて自らの責任を果たすために，自らが提供するものを有意義かつ記憶に残る文脈の中に位置づける必要がある。

6.4.2 MLAの戦略設定

Porter（2007）は，博物館部門の競争戦略に関する自らの理論をさらに練り上げ，博物館組織は公益を促進し得るが，慈善活動や寄付を通じた地域社会への奉仕は誤った考え方であると指摘した。むしろ，社会サービスの提供，「顧客」のニーズを満たすこと，そして高い価値を実現することなどが正しい目標であるとしている。

良いことを行うには良い戦略が必要となる。最も重要なステップは適切な目標を定義することであり，これが定まれば，後は重要な質問（サービスを提供する場所，提供するサービスの内容，提供方法，それらのサービスを地域社会開発の目標と合わせる方法）に答える中でMLAの運営が定まるだろう。MLAの義務は，社会的利益を最大限に生み出す一方で，関与するリソースを最小限に抑えられる方法で社会的価値を創造することである。定義，評価，報告は，戦略的構想を実施するための3つの基本ステップである。

以下に，概念的に欠陥のある考え方のトップ3を挙げる[5]。

1. 「強い願望としての戦略：我々の戦略は，1,000家族に奉仕し，250人の雇用を創出し（後略）」
2. 「行動としての戦略：我々の戦略は，新しい建物を建て（中略）家族に対する10万ドルの支援を行うことである」
3. 「ビジョン／使命としての戦略：我々の戦略は，地域社会に貢献し（中略）慈善精神を示すことである」

戦略とは，対象となる受益者／顧客に対して最大限の社会的価値を創出するための全体的なアプローチである。博物館の社会サービスの目標を設定するには，達成すべき社会的利益を特定し，十分に検討することが必要となる。実際には，非営利組織たる博物館にとって，目標の定義と戦略とは不可分に結びついている。

6.5 MLA と 21 世紀型スキル：アメリカにおける博物館・図書館サービス機構（IMLS）の構想

6.5.1 インターネットがもたらしたもの

ユーティリティネットワークを介して提供されるクラウドベースの技術が幅広く展開されたことで，オンラインビデオやリッチメディアが急成長した。現在では，データネットワークが無限に近い容量をもち，ほぼ無料となることが期待されている。インターネットを触媒として利用することによって，私たちは常に教育だけでなく非公式学習についても見直す必要に迫られている。

トーマス・フリードマン，マイケル・マンデルバウムの共著『かつての超大国アメリカ：どこで間違えたのか，どうすれば復活できるのか』（2011）では，アメリカが今日直面している4つの重大な問題，すなわちグローバリゼーション，IT革命，巨額の財政赤字，およびエネルギー消費の増加と，その解決策を取り上げている。先見性のある2人の著者は，新たな学習の生態系と，こうした新たな環境において21世紀型スキルが重要となる理由を述べている。

> 成長するためには，まだ存在しない仕事をするように人々を教育しなければならない。つまり，そうした仕事を創出すると同時に，人々がそれを行えるよう訓練しなければならない。これはさらに困難な作業であるため，誰もが創造的なクリエイターもしくは創造的な仕える人を目指すことが求められている[6]。

6.5.2 21 世紀型スキル構想が発展した経緯

官民パートナーシップの尽力により，2002年に21世紀型スキルのためのパートナーシップ（「P21」）が誕生した。その使命は，教育，ビジネス，地域社会，および政府首脳の間で協力的なパートナーシップを構築することで，アメリカがK–12教育において21世紀への対応力を高めるための触媒としての役割を果たすことである（FRIEDMAN, 2011）。将来に向けて世界的に競争力

図1　21世紀型スキル開発の成果とリソース
出典：Framework of P21 Skills.[7]

のある人材を育成するために，P21計画では，アメリカの教室内の環境と実世界の環境とをうまく調和させるための根幹として「3R」と「4C」を特定している。3R（Reading, Writing, Arithmetic　読み，書き，算数）には，英語，読書または言語技術，数学，科学，外国語，公民，政治学，経済，芸術，歴史，地理が含まれる。4Cには，批判的思考と問題解決，コミュニケーションとコラボレーション，および創造力とイノベーションが含まれる。

　3Rが他の科目やコアコンテンツを保護する力として役立つのに対して，4Cには，学業や職業，そして人生における成功に必要とされるあらゆるスキルが集約されている。図1では，P21の対象となる学生に向けた半円形の枠組みは，21世紀に必要とされる多次元的な能力を習得するための革新的な支援体制と融合した，特定のスキル，知識の内容，専門知識，およびリテラシーを示している。

6.5.3　IMLSが21世紀型スキル構想を導入した理由

　連邦政府機関である博物館・図書館サービス機構（IMLS）は，図書館や博物館が，助成金，研究，政策展開，および国家的パートナーシップを通じて，

イノベーション，生涯学習，そして市民の文化活動への参加を促進するよう奨励している。「今日の社会で成功するためには，情報リテラシー，自立精神，そして高いコラボレーション能力やコミュニケーション能力，問題解決力が不可欠である。伝統的な学習における強みと現代のコミュニケーションインフラへの活発な投資を組み合わせることで，図書館や博物館は21世紀にアメリカ人が必要とするスキルを磨くための十分な備えを整えることができる」[8]。

図書館や博物館は，21世紀において求められるものを考慮し，現在の強みを踏まえつつ新たなアプローチを採用すべきである。その一例を表2に挙げる。

表2　博物館・図書館・アーカイブズの変容

20世紀型　博物館／図書館	21世紀型　博物館／図書館
主にコンテンツ主導型	利用者とコンテンツ主導との組み合わせ
有形物が主体	有形物およびデジタル資料
一方通行	多方向
紹介や展示を重視	利用者の参加や体験を重視
独立して活動	密接なパートナーシップにより活動
地域社会の中に位置している	地域社会の中に組み込まれている
想定され，暗示される学習成果	目的を達成するための学習成果

出典：IMLS（2008）. Museums, Libraries and 21st Century Skills. Washington, DC: Institute of Museum and Library Services IMLS, p. 7.[9]

6.6　教訓

P21プログラムは，官民パートナーシップ（PPP）プログラムとして，将来の労働力を養成するための全方位的な枠組みを2002年から首尾よく開発してきた。教育と市民参加に関して博物館と図書館を支援するアメリカ連邦機関であるIMLSは，直ちに自らのガイドラインをこのプログラムに便乗させることによって，MLA部門をP21プログラムに参加させた。同プログラムが10年間展開された結果，アメリカはイノベーションを通じて世界経済をリードしてい

る。P21プログラムは，社会的・経済的発展に大きな役割を果たしたのである。

別の記述にもあるように，アメリカにおけるこうした教育重視の構想については，レーガン政権下で設置された，教育の卓越性に関する国家委員会の報告書「危機に立つ国家：教育改革のための命題」（1983）が契機となった。同報告書は，かつては商業，産業，科学，技術革新の卓越性を誇り確固たる地位を築いていたアメリカが，世界中の競争相手に追い越される危機に瀕していると指摘し，Paul Coppermanの言葉を引用している。それによれば，アメリカではこれまで各世代が教育，識字率，経済的達成度において親世代に勝ってきたが，史上初めて特定世代の教育スキルが親世代のそれを上回ったり，匹敵したり，近づくことさえできない状況になるという。

アメリカの人々は，この新たな時代に欠かせないスキル，リテラシー，トレーニングのレベルをもたない者は，優れた業績に伴う物的な報酬だけでなく，国民生活に十分に参加する機会を事実上奪われることを知る必要がある。自由で民主的な社会のためには，そして共通文化の育成には，高いレベルでの教育を共有することが不可欠である。特に多元主義と個人の自由を誇るアメリカのような国においては。

知識，学習，情報，そしてスキルを伴う知性は国際商取引の新たな素材であり，今日ではかつて特効薬や合成肥料，ブルージーンズなどがそうであったように，活発に世界中に広がっている。同報告書は「高校のカリキュラムにおける新たな5つの基礎科目」を，①英語，②数学，③科学，④社会科，⑤コンピュータサイエンス，と定義している。大学入学のために，高校でさらに2年間外国語を学習することが強く勧められている。

「危機に立つ国家」（1983）で述べられた高校での基礎5教科をベースに，また2002年以来の「3Rおよび4Cの21世紀型スキルに向けたパートナーシップ」を通して，アメリカのMLA部門は，社会に役立つ非公式学習の生態系において，重要な役割を果たしてきた。

終わりに，以下に挙げるアメリカ博物館協会（AAM）の倫理規定が，博物館の社会的使命についての適切な全体像を私たちに提供してくれるだろう。

第6章　情報科学による市民のエンパワーメント

　全体として，博物館のコレクションや展示資料は，世界の自然と文化の共有財産を表すものである。博物館は，その財産の担い手として，あらゆる自然の形態や人間の経験に対する理解を促進することが求められる。人類が継承した豊かで多様な世界について人々が十分な情報を得た上で評価できるよう，博物館は人類とそのあらゆる活動のための資源となる義務がある[10]。

注・引用文献

1 ：Statista (2017). Social Media Top 5 Social Media Networks Account for 6 Billion Users in 2017 <https://www.statista.com/statistics/272014/global-social-networks-ranked-by-number-of-users/>
2 ：TAPSCOTT, Don (2010). "Rethinking in a Netw or why Michael Porter is wrong about Internet," *Strategy + Bussiness,* issue 24, p. 5.
3 ：You – Yes, You – Are TIME's Person of the Year. <http://content.time.com/time/magazine/article/0,9171,1570810,00.html>
4 ：ICOM Statutes, Approved in Vienna (Austria) August 24, 2007, p. 2. <http://icom.museum/fileadmin/user_upload/pdf/Statuts/statutes_eng.pdf>
5 ：PORTER, Michael (2007). Doing Well at Doing Good: Do You Have a Strategy? Willow Creek Association Leadership Summit South Barrington, Illinois, August 10, 2007 <http://www.hbs.edu/faculty/Pages/item.aspx?num=46838>
6 ：ibid., p. 137.
7 ：Framework of P21 Skills <http://www.p21.org/about-us/p21-framework>
8 ：IMLS (2008). Museums, Libraries and 21st Century Skills. Washington, DC: Institute of Museum and Library Services IMLS <https://www.imls.gov/assets/1/AssetManager/21stCenturySkills.pdf>
9 ：ibid., p. 7.
10：AAM. Code of Ethics for Museums. Arlington VA, U.S.A.: American Alliance of Museums, 2000 <http://aam-us.org/resources/ethics-standards-and-best- practices/code-of-ethics>

参考文献

AAM. Code of Ethics for Museums. Arlington VA, U.S.A.: American Alliance of Museums, 2000. <http://aam-us.org/resources/ethics-standards-and-best- prac-

tices/code-of-ethics>

DICKER, Erika (2010). The Impact of Blogs and Other Social Media on the Life of a Curator, Museums and the Web 2010 – the international conference for culture and heritage on-line, Denver, Colorado, USA, April 13-17. <http://www.museumsandtheweb.com/mw2010/papers/dicker/dicker.html#ixzz29dROR oyN>

Framework of P21 Skills <http://www.p21.org/about-us/p21-framework>

FRIEDMAN, Thomas and MANDELBAUM, Michael (2011). *That Used to Be Us: How America Fell Behind in the World It Invented and How We Can Come Back*. New York, U.S.A.: Farrar, Straus and Giroux.

IMLS (2008). Museums, Libraries and 21st Century Skills. Washington, DC: Institute of Museum and Library Services IMLS <https://www.imls.gov/assets/1/AssetManager/21stCenturySkills.pdf>

IMLS (2013). Annual Report Number of Museums and Libraries, Washington <https://www.imlsProceeedings....gov/sites/default/files/publications/documents/2013annualreport_0.pdf>

National Commission on Excellence in Education (1983). *A Nation at Risk*, Washington D.C., the U.S. Department of Education <https://files.eric.ed.gov/fulltext/ED226006.pdf>

Nielson (2009). Global Faces and Network Places: A Nelson Report on Social Networking's New Global Footprints, Nielson Company <http://www.nielsen.com/us/en/insights/reports/2009/Social-Networking-New-Global-Footprint.html>

PORTER, Michael (2007). Doing Well at Doing Good: Do You Have a Strategy? Willow Creek Association Leadership Summit South Barrington, Illinois, August 10, 2007 <http://www.hbs.edu/faculty/Pages/item.aspx?num=46838>

Statista (2017). Social Media Top 5 Social Media Networks Account for 6 Billion Users in 2017 <https://www.statista.com/statistics/272014/global-social-networks-ranked-by-number-of-users/>

TAPSCOTT, Don (2010). Rethinking in a Netw or why Michael Porter is wrong about Internet, *Strategy + Bussiness,* issue 24, p. 1-8. <https://faculty.darden.virginia.edu/ebusiness/Tapscott%20Article.pdf>

Wang, L. (2009). "Building Conscience Driven Culture by Regional Heritage – Social Mission of Museums for the 21st Century," Proceeding of ICOM ASPAC TOKYO, 2009.

あとがき
情報を知性へと変換すること，知性を英知へと変換すること

　本書をまとめるにあたって，思ったほど多くの内容をカバーできていなかったことを痛切に感じた。と同時に，何度も繰り返し同様のテーマを取り上げ，紙面を費やしすぎたかもしれない。では，筆者が最も語りたかったことは何であろうか。

　まず，頭に思い浮かぶキーワードは，知識，生涯学習，市民のエンパワーメント，第三次産業革命，科学，哲学，そして宗教。アルベルト・アインシュタインが述べたとおり，「宗教無き科学は欠陥であり，科学無き宗教は盲目」である。欠陥や盲目にならないための，微妙な境界線が存在する。筆者はこれが，本書の執筆の端緒だと考える。先の道のりは長いだろう。読者の皆様からの励ましや助言を引き続き得て，今後も情報を知性に変換し，知性を英知へと変換する方法の探究を続けていくことができれば，大変ありがたく思う。

　筆者は，この世には運命が存在すると信じている。そして筆者自身の運命は筑波山に関連していると思う。初めて訪れたのは，国際博物館会議アジア太平洋地域連盟（ICOM ASPAC）日本会議で初めて発表を行った2009年のことであった。以来，シカゴ市とつくば市という「二都」を往復して暮らしている。筆者が博士課程進学のために最良の大学院を探す際にも，博物館分野での筆者の職業と北米‐アジアの地域社会の発展を追究することは，西洋と東洋への独特の視点を与えてくれた。

　次に示す「筑波大学図書館情報メディア研究科パンフレット2017‐2018」に寄稿した文章を結びの言葉としたい。

理想のカリキュラム，理想の大学，理想の場所

　私は，筑波大学大学院図書館メディア情報研究科を愛している。「情報を知性に変換する」という先駆的な探究の場だからである。周知のとおり，第三次産業革命は，私たちの伝統的な学習方法にも多大な影響を与えている。本校の

構造組織は，学際的な教育と多文化研究を促進するものであり，本校の幹部や教職員は，明確に定義された学問的境界をもつ独立した研究分野から，さまざまな分野の参加者が連携する共同ネットワークへの転換を試みている。

ビッグデータの時代にあって，現象の研究に対する伝統的な方法論に代わり，現実の性質と存在の意味についての全体像の問題が体系的に追究され始めている。私の博士論文は，情報科学による市民のエンパワーメント－情報化時代における社会発展のための博物館，図書館，アーカイブズの変化の傾向に焦点を当てている。

私は筑波大学を愛している。将来のグローバルリーダーたちに，その可能性をすべて実現させる環境を提供することを最優先の使命と位置づけているからである。世界中の最先端研究によって裏打ちされた教育を通して，学生に個性とスキルを育てる機会を与えてくれる。多様なグローバルリーダーシップ・プログラムは，グローバリゼーションの現象を背景に集団で取り組まれてきた開発を通して人類を良い方向へ導くための才能と見識を提供してくれる。

私は筑波研究学園都市を愛している。イノベーション精神が根づいているからである。科学研究機関が一地域に集中することで，産学官連携を推進し，教育・研究能力の強化を図りつつ，積極的に社会に貢献することができる。過去数十年の間に，基礎研究における政府と産業界の連携のための世界的拠点のひとつとなった。筑波研究学園都市は，第二のシリコンバレーと呼ばれている。

社会発展の主な原動力は，政治，経済，知識，メディアである。現在は古い産業社会の時代から新しい情報社会の時代への移行期にあり，ソーシャルメディア，デジタルモビリティ，クラウドコンピューティング，そしてビッグデータが人々の働き方や考え方さえも変えつつある。私は，最終教育課程を修了できるという素晴らしい機会を得たことに感謝している。また筑波大学で実に豊かな経験を得られことは，非常に幸運であった。

私の研究も「情報を知性へと変換」し，やがて研究者の一人として知性を普遍的な英知へと変換していきたいと考えている。

2018 年 2 月

王　莉

Empowerment of Citizens
Social Mission and Functions of Museums and
Libraries in the 21st Century

Introduction
A Nation At Risk
An American Tale for Lifelong Learning

While conducting research on empowerment of citizens with informatics, I was exposed to enormous amounts of information on U.S. educational policy I was shocked when I read a 1983 white paper, ***A Nation at Risk,*** on education published by the U.S. Congress. The report was compiled by President Ronald Regan's National Commission of Excellence in Education. At that time, there existed only two super powers in the world, the Soviet Union and the United States. Why was the U.S. a nation at risk to an act of war, and from whom?

> *If an unfriendly foreign power had attempted to impose on America the mediocre educational performance that exists today, we might well have viewed it as an act of war. As it stands, we have allowed this to happen to ourselves. We have even squandered the gains in student achievement made in the wake of the Sputnik challenge.*[1]

The report stated the American prosperity, security and civility have been eroded by a rising tide of mediocrity in education. It revealed the fact that America's previously unchallenged preeminence in commerce, industry, science, and technological innovation was overtaken by competitors throughout the world. Knowledge, learning, information, and skilled intelligence would soon become the new raw materials of international commerce and replace what miracle drugs, synthetic fertilizers, and blue jeans contributed to the world in the past.

Historically, events have always been surprisingly identical. "A Tale of Twin Cities" painted a picture on the eve of the Second Industrial Revolution:

> *It was the best of times, it was the worst of times, it was the age of wisdom,*

Introduction A Nation At Risk

it was the age of foolishness, it was the epoch of belief, it was the epoch of incredulity, it was the season of Light, it was the season of Darkness, it was the spring of hope, it was the winter of despair, we had everything before us, we had nothing before us...[2]

On the eve of the Third Industrial Revolution, American visionary leaders called to the public attention that a learning society is needed to face a changing world of ever-accelerating competition in the workplace, of ever-greater danger, and of ever-larger opportunities. This learning society is the fundamental commitment to a set of values and to a system of education that affords all members the opportunity to stretch their minds to full capacity for lifelong learning.

The learning society shall consist of not only traditional institutions such as schools and colleges, but also libraries, art galleries, museums, and science centers. The goal of education is to meet all individuals' goals for career and to add value to their lives. A high level of shared education is essential to a free, democratic society and to the fostering of a common culture, especially in a country that prides itself on pluralism and individual freedom.

Formal learning during youth is the essential foundation for learning throughout our life. The future quality of life requires lifelong learning as individuals' skills become rapidly outdated in the information age. Americans considered education more important than developing the best industrial system or the strongest military force. They understood education as the cornerstone of financial and military might.

The report recommended that state and local high school graduation requirements be strengthened and that, at a minimum, all students seeking a diploma be required to lay the foundations in the Five New Basics by determining competence in English, mathematics, science, social studies, and computer science. For the college-bound, two years of foreign language in high school are strongly recommended in addition to any foreign language classes taken earlier.

America knows that education is one of the driving engines of a society's material well-being. Education is the common bond of our modern society and helps tie us to other cultures around the globe. America knows that the security of the United States depends principally on the wit, skill, and spirit of a self-confident people; today and tomorrow.

I have used this report as a guideline for why we need to be actively engaged in lifelong learning, how we use museums and libraries as the extended space for citizens' development, and goals for achieving social development by way of social mission and public services roles of museums and libraries.

Beyond Time, Beyond Space and Beyond Ourselves — Onion Peeling Process of My Study

This book is a collection of my papers published since 2009. It is a step by step foot print recording my study on lifelong learning from a museum educator's perspective on the role and social mission of museums, libraries and archives. These papers reflect my comparative research conducted by application of the sociology of case museum and library studies in the U.S., U.K., Japan and China.

Previously, I was a learning and development officer for international exchange in a famous oriental history museum. During my first six-year career right after college, I acquainted a few hundred international dignitaries from all over the world. I was constantly challenged by intelligent questions from those leaders covering issues such as politics, religion, trade associations, and international exchange agencies. So many visitors inspired my thinking of how to use the history as a mirror to viewing the root cause of the global financial crisis of 2008. Like most millennials at that time, I did not pay much attention to community development issues. Reading the ***Language of Conscience***, a book written by an American banker, I was inspired to transform from a seasonal museum fellow to a PhD candidate at the Graduate School of Library, Information and Media at the University of Tsukuba.

The articles included in this book are organized in such a way each is self-contained material for a specific angle from which to view the mission and public service roles of museums and libraries, with the ultimate goal to empower citizens with informatics.

Building Conscience-Driven Culture Based on Regional Heritage: Social Mission of Museums for the 21st Century [Social Mission Perspective]

This was my first academic paper presented at ICOM ASPAC Tokyo 2009.

Introduction A Nation At Risk

While attempting to understand what happened to our community as a result of the failure of the Wall Street financial market in 2008, I learned that a lack of conscience-based fundamental values could be one of the major root cause reasons.

Generally, we consider the main functions of a museum to include research, collection, storage, exhibition, education etc. In today's world, our challenge is determining first how to transform the public's perception from viewing a museum as a tourism attraction to a source of regional heritage conservation and promotion; and second how to create a systematic approach for museum professionals as knowledge brokers to build a conscience-driven culture by regional heritage.

Viewing museums as a house for knowledge brokering, a full spectrum end-to-end process development should be introduced to cover the whole life cycle of knowledge brokering. The process can be classified into the stages of: Creating, Acquiring, Assimilating, Using, and Disseminating Knowledge.

The internet and information technology not only changed our traditional way of learning, but also made an impact on our fundamental values. Today, commercialized media and information sources shape values through entertainment and convenience. How to apply modern technology to economic development, together with core value creation has become a critical mission for world civilization today.

Although it is such a great challenge to promote culture, which by its nature is intangible, the network of museums are the tangible venue not only to link our past, present and future, but also link with other nations through conscience. Museums and libraries are expressions of cultural Identity in our modern society.

Building a conscience-driven culture by regional heritage as the historic social mission of museums for the 21st Century came to my mind during my initial exploration.

Challenges & Opportunities in Museum Development: A Historic-Sociological Perspective — China versus Japan [Sociology and Economic Perspective]

I presented this article at ICOM CECA 2011 in Zegrab, Croatia. I conducted research to link social development with museum growth in order to understand roles museums may play for our society with comparative study on Japan and China.

As of 2010, after three decades of open policy, China surpassed Japan as the world's second-largest economy. At the same time, the number of museums in China increased ten-fold from 300 to 3,000. While over a nearly 60 year period in Japan, the number of museums increased nearly 35 times from 145 in 1945 to 5,000 in 2003.

Past events of museum development in comparison with economic development by time and territory dimensions in Japan and China were investigated by application of historic — sociology methodology. Qualitative and quantitative methods were combined for such historical-comparative study. The goal for this project was to use time, people, community, social and economic development elements to understand museum roles in education and innovation.

For easy comparison purposes, five stage approaches were created to view how Japan developed their social education system by utilizing museums to address issues faced by other similar industrial nations such as how China developed its museum system in combination with its record high economic growth.

The five stage comparison between China and Japan includes: initiation by administration versus academic society driven; economic growth by public education versus political mass movement; maturity by landmark development versus culture relics protection; myth by museum pathology versus hardware building; and future by performance management versus social mission. Innovation will be the dominant factor to drive the future in the 21st Century. Studies by the U.S., U.K. and Australian governments illustrate that museum roles, education, culture and art, innovation, social and economic development are intricately related. Knowledge of social studies will impact the public to inspire innovation for social and economic development.

Museum 2.0: An Extended Exhibition in Cyberspace by Social Media [Digitalization and Change Management Perspective]

This article was pesented at ICOM CECA 2012 in Yerevan, Armenia. I was the first to put forth the ideas of Museum 2.0 and its impact via social media at the CECA conference.

Introduction A Nation At Risk

The key drivers of social development are generally considered as Politics, Economy, Knowledge and Media. We are in a transition from an old era, an industrial society, to a new era, an information society. Today, social media, digital mobility and cloud computing are changing the ways people are thinking and working.

The museum 5G theory by Dr. Mizushima was a first of its kind description of museum development in the world: Museum 1G as Collection; Museum 2G as Conservation; Museum 3G as Exhibition & Education; Museum 4G as Digitization for Input/Output; and Museum 5G as Converter for Participation.

From the current development of cloud computing and social media, the author believes the age of the sixth generation of museum has arrived; Museum 6G as Center for Excellence of Culture Resources Integration and Management.

The process ownership perspective of 6G museum research dimension reveals who will be the process owners for the CHANGE of future museums. Traditionally, museum curators are the ones who lead all major efforts and activities for the change and development. Social media will influence public not only by what they want to see in the physical and digital museums, but also how they obtain information and how they transform information into knowledge.

It is the new global trend to view museums as the knowledge source of civilization with focal points of conscience, wisdom and art. The impact of social media has created tremendous challenges to museum educators in this information age.

The Glory and the Dream: Rethinking the Social Mission of Museums in the Era of Cyber Space [The Third Industrial Revolution Perspective]

In the early 20th century as farm jobs became mechanized, there was less need for farm labor. Some decades later, manufacturing jobs became mechanized and there was less need for factory labor. Now business processes — many in the service sector — are becoming mechanized, requiring fewer people which is exerting systematic downward pressure on jobs and lower skilled employment.

As one of the key growth engines of the 21st Century, the second economy is creating prosperity without creating complimentary job opportunities. Our society is facing a huge challenge of how to distribute instead of producing prosperity. As we traditionally believe, wealth should be associated with labor. As we reduced agriculture jobs, we created manufacturing jobs. Furthermore, we are phasing out blue-collar manufacturing jobs and replacing them with white-collar service jobs. With this digital transformation, this last repository of jobs is shrinking — fewer of us in the future may have white-collar business process jobs — so we are faced with a significant social problem.

I have been researching what Japan did while other industrial nations were transforming from building "muscular systems" to developing "neural systems" over the last three decades. In building its muscular system, Japan established many primary brands, such as Toyota, as dominant global powers in manufacturing. Even Americans are learning from Toyota not only in terms of technology and innovation, but also from its management system. However, how can Japan maintain this strength? Japan used to be the leader in ICT information communication technology. Japan should create its own "Apple" like Korea did with Samsung to compete with America's Apple. Most recently, the downgrading of Sony and Panasonic's credit rating to near junk status shows how Japan's leadership position in innovation is deteriorating rapidly.

Japan built up its powerful "muscular system" in the industrial age through the development of Toyota. Japan will rebuild its past glory through companies like Sony/Panasonic to achieve a powerful "neural system" in transitioning to the information age.

Digital Engagement as a Catalyst in Transforming Museums, Libraries and Archives: A Case Study of the Field Museum of Natural History [Best Practice in the U.S.]

This was the invited paper for 2017 Journal of Japan Museum Management Academy. I presented the case study of the Field Museum of Natural History in Chicago as a show and tell case for the best practice as museum's social mission and social service roles.

The Field Museum of Natural History in Chicago is one of the largest natural history museums in the world. The museum maintains its premier status through the size and quality of its educational and scientific programs. The

Introduction   A Nation At Risk

Field Museum itself is a 3-in-1 Museum Library and Archive facility occupying a building space of 80,000 square meters. Its collection center is host to 24.7 million specimens, with 200,000 items added each year. Its library has 275,000 books, 278 subscriptions to domestic and foreign journals, 1,800 feet of archival records, 7,500 rare books, and 3,000 works of art. Its photo archives consist of 300,000 images. Annually, the Field Museum attracts 800-900 visiting professors and research scientists, as well as two million on-site visitors from all continents.

The Field Museum is not an isolated case. The phenomenon is well rooted in the U.S. political, economic, and cultural soil. In the U.S., there are 123,000 libraries and 17,500 museums. The Institute of Museum and Library Services (IMLS) is a federal government agency which seeks to encourage libraries and museums to advance innovation, lifelong learning, and cultural and civic engagement through grant making, research, policy development and national partnerships. IMLS assists museums and libraries offer engaging learning experiences, enabling them to be strong community anchors, aiding in the care of museum and library collections, and promoting use of technology to increase access to content.

The Field Museum, The Museum of Science + Industry, The Art Institute of Chicago, Chicago Central Library, and the National Archives at Chicago are world class institutions. They are leading innovation and change in the museums and libraries.

Empowerment of Citizens with Informatics: Museums, Libraries and Archives in Cyberspace [The Utmost Goal for Museums and Libraries to Serve the Public]

This article was the published for the Museology and Heritage Journal in Brazil. The speed and magnitude of the development and innovation in cyberspace over the last two decades is transforming how we live, work and think. "Smart" devices, such as the iPhone, have facilitated the retrieval and sharing of information before, during and after a visit to an MLA (Museum, Library, and Archive) location.

Lessons are being drawn from the history of adult education to promote community development to help museums face challenges in dealing with the wave of information technology. U.S. public policy on education and its goal to build 21st century skills is examined to review its impact on the social mission of the MLA sector.

To develop a globally competitive workforce for the future, the P21 initiative identifies the 3Rs and 4Cs as core elements to successfully align the U.S. classroom environment with the real-world environment. The 3Rs (Reading, Writing and Arithmetic) include: English, reading or language arts; mathematics; science; foreign languages; civics; government; economics; arts; history; and geography. The 4Cs include: critical thinking and problem solving; communication and collaboration; and creativity and innovation.

While the 3Rs serve as an umbrella for other subjects and core content, the 4Cs are a shorthand for all the skills needed for success in college, in your career, and in life.

In the 21st century, citizens have more leisure time to enjoy life and engage in lifelong learning programs for their professional development. As MLAs are increasingly focusing attention on audience development and better service to their visitors. These potential audiences are deluged by an increasing volume of information and numerous channels bringing choice between leisure time and learning opportunities. Thus, rising public participation in MLAs is being challenged by increasing competition. And, MLAs need to position their offerings in a context that is both meaningful and memorable in order to fulfill their social mission responsibilities.

This book is written for the purpose to share my own learning on lifelong learning and empowerment of citizens with informatics. It can be used by educational professionals in museums, libraries, lifelong learning institutions, and not for profit organizations such as healthcare entities to promote "out of the box" thinking to reach out to citizens for lifelong learning.

Note

1 : National Commission on Excellence in Education (1983). *A Nation at Risk,* Washington D.C., the U.S. Department of Education, p. 9. <https://files.eric.ed.gov/fulltext/ED226006.pdf>
U.S. Government have this sort of electronic publication.

2 : Charles Dickens (2003). *A Tale of Two Cities,* Random House Publishing Group, p. 6.

1

Building Conscience-Driven Culture Based on Regional Heritage

Social Mission of Museums for the 21st Century

The world-renowned sociologist Fei Xiaotong said, "The day, when every nation values the merit of heritage of its own, respects the merit of heritage of others, and shares the merit of heritage with all, is the day of world harmony.[1]" Fei's remarks were made at his birthday party thrown by Professor Chie Nakane in Tokyo in December 1990. It is amazing how historic events repeat themselves. Almost two decades later, we are here to share the same vision Fei and Nakane presented through the theme of this conference, "Rethinking the Core Value of Museums and Regional Heritage."

Building a conscience-driven culture based on regional heritage has become the historic social mission of museums for the 21st Century. When we seek to understand what happened to our community due to the failure of Wall Street, it is easy to see how a lack of fundamental conscience-based values could be one of the major causes of this tragedy. The following quotes may help us have perspective on the issue.

> *When the people of the world all know beauty as beauty, there arises the recognition of ugliness. When they all know good as good, there arises the recognition of evil.*
> — *Lao-tzu*
>   *The Way of Lao-tzu I*[2]
>
> *He who wishes to secure the good of others has already secured his own.*
> — *Confucius*[3]
>
> *This is the noble Eightfold way: Namely right view, right intention, right speech, right action, self-livelihood, right effort, right mindfulness, right concentration. This monks, is a Middle Path, of which the Taghagata (the*

Buddha) has gained enlightenment, which provides insight and knowledge, and tends to calm, to higher knowledge, enlightenment, Nirvana.
  — *Buddha (Siddhartha Butama)*
  The Sermon at Benares[4]

It is not an easy task to realize the vision presented by Fei and Nakane. The internet and information technology not only changed our traditional way of learning, but made an impact on our fundamental values. Today, our values are shaped by commercialized media and information sources for our entertainment and convenience. Much attention has been paid to developing natural resources through government and business initiatives. Less attention has been paid to developing human resources. It is a fact that a nation which pays attention to the development of human resources can have great economic success even without adequate natural resources. How to apply modern technology for the sake of economic development in addition to core value creation has become a critical mission for world civilization today.

We are living in a world of globalization. As we all know, it is very hard to use something other than culture, such as politics or economics, as a bridge for cross-cultural communication due to the complexities of nationalism, religion and self-interest on a region by region basis. Culture could be the key conduit to instil values which transcend generations. Although it is a great challenge to promote culture, as it is by its very nature intangible, a network of museums could be a tangible way to link the past, present and future, as well as to link our conscience with other nations.

The Coalition Sites of Conscience is a good case in point for us to review how we might carry the social mission of museums forward in the 21st century. It is a network of historic site museums in many countries. They share the following belief:

> *...it is the obligation of historic sites to assist the public in drawing connections between the history of our sites and their contemporary implications. We view stimulating dialogue on pressing social issues and promoting humanitarian and democratic values as a primary function.*[5]

Chapter 1 Building Conscience-Driven Culture Based on Regional Heritage

We need to develop non-profit organizations represented by museums to promote public awareness of citizens' social responsibilities. Education in ethics, morality, conscience, integrity and character will have an effect on the culture that ultimately changes our civilization. As a museum professional, what we have done or how well we have done it is not that important. However, it is very important for us to know why we need to do what we have done.

We normally consider the main functions of a museum to include research, collection, storage, exhibition, and education etc. According to Wikipedia's definition, the word "museum" comes from the Latin word denoting a place or temple dedicated to the Muses (the patron divinities of the arts in Greek mythology), and hence a building set apart for study and the arts, especially a Musaeum (institute) for philosophy and research.

The first challenge we are facing is how to transform the public's perception of a museum as a tourist attraction, into a source of regional heritage and its conservation and promotion. The general public will be let down without understanding the true value of the museum. This has become a serious issue for stakeholders in the public such as community and business leaders, educators, government officials as well as politicians. Not long ago, the Chinese government phased out admission fees to major national and local museums to offer better access to the general public. However, there is limited training for museum professionals and little information available on how to educate museum visitors adequately on its value.

The second challenge we are facing is how to create a systematic approach for museum professionals as knowledge brokers to build a conscience-driven culture based on regional heritage.

Viewing museums as a venue for knowledge brokering, a full spectrum end-to-end process should be introduced to cover the whole life-cycle of developing knowledge brokering. This process can be broken down into the stages of: Creating, Acquiring, Assimilating, Using, and Disseminating Knowledge.

Professional development of our back-end research and support staff as well as learning and development staff in dealing with the public is urgently needed. It could be a great initiative for ICOM — ASPAC to develop a curriculum and workshops with standardized processes, methodology and accreditation for the knowledge brokering process with the collaboration of our member museums.

In conclusion, a comprehensive public-private partnership beyond boarders should be created to call the attention of all stakeholders to the importance of safeguarding our regional heritage to create a harmonious world. Using a systematic approach will help museums develop knowledge brokering systems as the means to fulfill our social mission for the 21st century, which is to relay our nation's unique heritage while at the same time integrating with others.

Note

1：费孝通(2013), 全球化与文化自觉 ：费孝通晚年文选, 北京, 外语教学与研究出版社, p. 6-16.
   This book has no official English translation.
2：Lin YuTang (2009). *Chinese-English Bilingual Edition: The Wisdom of Laotse (1)* (Bilingual literature, Volume 1), Taipei, Cheng Chung Book Co., Ltd; 2nd edition (2009), p. 60.
3：Bell, D. (2000). *East Meets West: Human Rights and Democracy in East Asia,* Princeton University Press, p. 244.
4：Price, J. (2010). *Sacred Scriptures of the World Religions: An Introduction,* Bloomsbury Academic, p. 58.
5：The International Coalition of Sites of Conscience <www.sitesofconscience.org>

2
Challenges & Opportunities in Museum Development
A Historic-Sociological Perspective — China versus Japan

As of 2010, China surpassed Japan as the world's second-largest economy after three decades of its open-door policy. At the same time, the number of museums in China increased from 300 in 1978 to 3,000 in 2010. In Japan, the number of museums increased from 145 in 1945 to 5,000 in 2003. Historical-Comparative Methodologies applied to study the public service roles of museums at different stages of economic development in Japan and China may reveal new perspectives on the impact of cultural development through regional economic growth. The five main characteristics of a comparison of Japan and China were:

1. initiation through government administration versus academic society
2. economic growth through public education versus mass political movements
3. maturity through development of landmarks versus the protection of cultural relics
4. myths stemming from museum pathology versus hardware building
5. building a future through performance management versus social mission

Innovation was the dominant factor driving future development for the 21st Century by examining Rostow's (1960) five-stage road map to industrialization with enhanced S-curve by Porter (2002). Studies by the U.S., the U.K. and the Australian governments illustrated that the roles of a museum are interrelated with education, culture and art, innovation, social and economic development. Knowledge of social studies will have public impact in spurring innovations for social and economic development.

2.1 Background: Economic Development Miracles in Japan and China

According to the World Development Indicators database on gross domestic product in 2010 released by the World Bank in July 2011, China produced $5.878,629 trillion and Japan produced 5.497,813 trillion U.S. dollars. Due to its open-door policy for the past three decades, China surpassed Japan as the world's second-largest economy in 2010. Figure 1 illustrates the trend in GDP growth over last two decades in Japan and China.

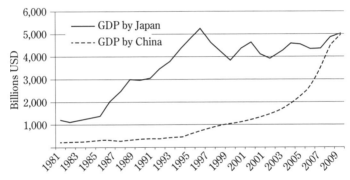

Figure 1. GDP Growth 1981 - 2009 Japan China
Data Source: World Bank1

Has China really surpassed Japan today? Table 1 reveals how China is still far behind Japan. However, there are many similarities between the two countries in terms of culture, heritage, social and economic development. A study on the lessons learned by the Japanese at different stages in their social development may help the Chinese in their own course of development. A study by W. Wang (2006) shows how China is facing serious challenges not only due to its huge population and lack of natural resources, but due to the lack of resources for humanity, which has generated created more obstacles to sustainable development of in China.

Table 1. Economy: Japan v.s. China

	Japan	China
Population (million)	126	1,336
Urban Population (2010)	67%	47%
Rate of Urbanization (2010 - 2015)	0.2%	2.3%
Area SQ KM	377,915	9,596,961
GDP Trillion USD (2010)	5,497	5,878
Growth Rate %	3.9%	10.3%
GDP Per Capita USD (2010)	34,000	7,600
GDP-by Sector		
Agriculture	1.4%	10.2%
Industry	24.9%	46.9%
Services	73.8%	43.0%
Labor Force Million (2010)	63	815
Labor Force by Sector		
Agriculture	3.9%	38.1%
Industry	26.2%	27.8%
Services	69.8%	34.1%

Data Source: CIA (2011). The World Fact book[2]

Thinking anew about the fundamental values of society and of China's cultural heritage could be two critical avenues to contribute to building a harmonious society. Over the last two decades, China's museum sector has been growing at a rapid pace together with the high growth rate of its national economy.

Figure 2 illustrates the trend in GDP growth rate compared with the number of museums in Japan and China. Seeing similar growth trends in GDP and museums in Japan and China, we tried to understand the challenges and opportunities in museum development for the twenty first century by studying this phenomenon through quantitative and qualitative analysis.

By its 12th Five Year Development Plan (2011 — 2015), China increased the number of its museums to 3,500, which amounted to 150 — 180 museums a year added over a four year period (SACH State Administration of Cultural Heritage, 2011). A methodology of combining a historic — sociological study and cultural economics is introduced in this study to understand the challenges and opportunities of museum development in Japan and China.

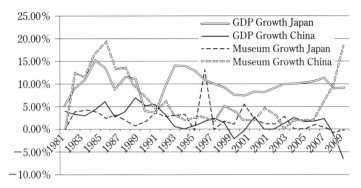

Figure 2. GDP Growth and Museum Growth Japan vs China
Data Source: World Bank (GDP)[3], MEXT (Japan Museum)[4], SACH (China Museum)[5]

2. 2 Social Mission of Museums

It is a new global trend to view museums as a source of knowledge for civilization which focuses on conscience, wisdom and art (Wang, 2009). According to the ICOM Statues adopted in Vienna in 2007, a museum is a "non-profit, permanent institution in the service of society and its development, open to the public, which acquires, conserves, researches, communicates and exhibits the tangible and intangible heritage of humanity and its environment for the purposes of education, study and enjoyment.[6]"

The ICOM Statues were initially drafted with a focus on collection and conservation, but were soon revised to include preserving, studying and enhancing in 1951. Education was added in 1961. Service to society and its development was added in 1974. Broader concepts were introduced to the museum definition in the 1989, 1995 and 2001 revisions. In 2007, education became the number one priority as a common goal for the fundamental services of museums, over and above "study and enjoyment." Together with this dynamic development of the museum's definition, the international museum community has been actively advocating and pursuing the social mission to build a harmonious society. The theme of ICOM-ASPAC Tokyo 2009 was "Rethinking the Core Values of Museums and Regional Heritage in the Asia-Pacific." The theme of ICOM Shanghai 2010 was "Museums and a Harmonious Society."

2.3 Museums, Innovation and Sustainable Social Development

In 2006, Professor Tony Travers of the London School of Economics conducted a study for the U.K. Museums, Libraries and Archives Council (MLA) and the National Museums Directors Conference (NMDC). In his report, Travers presented an updated analysis of a number of economic and social impacts of many of Britain's major museums and galleries. Museums played leading roles in encouraging civic development and economic regeneration within society. He found that, "the UK's museums and galleries could, with greater capacity to expand and improve, allow this country to be a world leader in creativity and scholarship.[7]" The report's positive findings included:

- *The economic benefits of the UK's major museums and galleries are estimated to be £1.5 billion per annum taking into account turnover and visitor expenditure. Broader economic impacts would be still greater;*
- *Generally speaking, £1 in every £1,000 in the UK economy can be directly related to the museum and gallery sector.*[8]

Cutler (2008) made clear a link from culture and art to economic development through his study on innovation. In his report, "Venturous Australia: Building Strength in Innovation" for the Ministry for Innovation, Industry, Science and Research, Cutler tried to make the point that there was a large gap between the way culture and the arts sees itself and formal innovation frameworks, policies and programs. This 202 page report not only studied other industrial nations, but also paid attention to emerging economies such as China and India. Believing that innovation is one of the key drivers of the 21st century, Cutler points out,"This is the innovative spirit we need to nurture in all Australians. An innovative Australia is a country that is enterprising and venturous.[9]"

As early as 1983, Americans realized that education is the key to maintaining its national competitiveness. "Our Nation is at Risk," a report by the The National Commission on Excellence in Education addressed how, "the educational foundations of our society are presently being eroded by a rising tide of mediocrity that threatens our very future as a Nation and a people...Our once unchallenged preeminence in commerce, industry, science, and technological innovation is being overtaken by competitors throughout the world. There could be many causes and dimensions of the problem, but education is the one that undergirds American prosperity, security, and civility.[10]" English, Math, Science, Social Studies and Computer Science are raised as the five fundamental skills for a high school education declaring, "Knowledge of the humanities, they maintain, must be harnessed to science and technology if the latter are to remain creative and humane.[11]"

Rostow (1960) created a five-stage model as a road map to explain how countries become industrialized. These five stages are:

1. the traditional society,
2. preconditions for takeoff,
3. economic takeoff,
4. the drive to maturity,
5. the age of mass consumption.[12]

This model works in most of the developed countries such as the U.K., the U.S, Canada, and Japan. As of today, the tertiary and quaternary industries are the two main sectors which will drive economic development in the 21st century. Both tertiary and quaternary industries are knowledge intensive, which requires innovation as the key driver.

2. 4　Lessons We May Learn from Japan and China

Past events in museum development in comparison with economic development by time and region in Japan and China were investigated by application of historic-sociological methodology. Qualitative and quantitative methods were combined for this historical-comparative study. The goal of this project is to use elements such as time, people, community, and social and economic development to understand the museum's role in education and innovation.

For easy comparison, a five-stage approach was created to visualize how

Japan developed its social education system by utilizing museums in dealing with similar issues like other industrial nations, and to understand how China developed its museum system together with its high economic growth.

Stage I: Modern Museum Initiation

Japan (1861 — 1951): Japan's operating model was "Administration-Driven." The Japanese government kicked off the initial establishment of museums nationwide from the administrative needs for national assets, natural resources, products, produce, and industrial information gathering for national policy on foreign trade and industrial development. Museums in Japan were born with the "DNA" for social economic development. In 1936, 320 museums were established including 10 in Korea and 10 in Taiwan.

China (1905 — 1936): China's operating model was "Academic Society -Driven." The academic community launched the museum to serve the needs of science and democracy in a new cultural movement. The China Museum Association was established in 1936 with conference proceedings. Museums in China were born with the "DNA" for cultural and academic development. In 1936, 77 museums were established including the Forbidden City Museum.

Stage II: Community Education Platform

Japan (1950 — 1969): Social education together with social and economic development was the main task carried out by museums. The Education Law, Social Education Law, Museum Law, Science Education Promotion Law, Industry Education Promotion Law were enacted in 1950 and 1951. According to Teuchi (2010), the Citizen Hall, the Library, and the Museum became the three key support columns of the Japanese Social Education System. Japan experienced high growth in its economic and social development. 1,670 museums opened from 1965 to 1977.

China (1949 — 1976): Museums became a national political education platform. Political propaganda along with socialist education was the main task carried out by museums. Developed upon the former Soviet Union model, building and operation, standards, architecture and the display design of museums were fully adopted from the USSR which was greatly influenced by political movements. The main focus of museums was on "class struggle." Society and culture were greatly damaged during the Cultural Revolution from 1966 through 1976. There were 72 museums in 1976.

Stage III: Growth with National Reform

Japan (1969 — 1989): Japan became the second largest economy by GDP in 1968 on the 100 anniversary ceremony of the Meiji Ishin (Meiji Restoration). Japan reached its peak in social and economic development. "Local," "Culture," and "Globalization" became themes for the building of new museums by local governments. Corporate memorial museums and art galleries became another social trend in museum development. Corporate culture became a buzz word in community development. 150 museums were added per year by the central government, local governments, and major corporations. The number of museums reached 3,289 in 1977.

China (1978 — 1990): Deng Xiaoping's open-door policy brought about the "New Spring of Chinese Museums." A chain of social and political events has changed China since then. Focus on the preservation of cultural relics became an important perspective on museum development. 100 — 120 museums were added per year by the central and local governments. Shaanxi History Museum was the first contemporary museum ever built in China. It took eight years from planning to completion (1983 — 1991).

Stage IV: Rethinking Museum Development

Japan (1990 — 2000): 200 museums were added by the central and local governments, as well as by communities. The vision and mission management of museums were lost in the high tide of museum development. This pathology of museums made the Japan Association of Museums aware of where they should go to institute reform. Public-Private Partnership (PPP) was introduced by "Mécénat" (Patronage) to provide support, encouragement, or financial aid to museums and art development. The public became aware of lifelong learning to prepare them for the 21st century.

China (1990 — 2010): 100 — 120 museums were added per year by the central and local governments as landmarks and symbols of urban development.

A real estate-driven economy made museums part of urbanization. Less consideration was placed on a museum's social mission and public service functions. Building hardware was the only issue and brought new challenges. China followed the footsteps taken by Japan in its similar "hardware" issues.

Stage V: Objective Driven Management

Japan (2000 —): The Japan Museum Management Academy (JMMA) developed a grading system for museum evaluation. Performance management was introduced by balanced scorecard and other methodologies. Digitalization, Dialogue and Communication for the social education of the public and for community participation were advocated. With educational reforms in 2002, an integrated study time initiative was commenced as part of social education for high school students.

China (2011 —): The state mission is to protect China's heritage and to build a spiritual homestead for everyone. 200 — 220 museums will be added per year by the central, local governments, and private investors. The social mission and public service roles are being reviewed by Chinese leadership. The innovation state, sustainable economy, green development, and cultural development are new dimensions of museum development. Social education by museums is being gradually recognized.

Japan is ahead of China in its operating mechanism to develop museums in line with its social mission. The Protection of Heritage and Building a Mutually Spiritual Homestead has become the social mission of the Chinese museum sector. Both Japan and China are pursuing improvement and excellence in operation still today.

2.5 Conclusion

For social development in the 21st century, it has been a great challenge and opportunity for museums to consider the enhancement of their public services functions as their social mission. It is the historic mission of our museum colleagues to protect our cultural heritage and to build our spiritual homeland by application of world-class best practice. Over the last three decades, devel-

Table 2. Evolution Process of Museum System in Japan and China

Stages	Museums Development	Japan	China
I	Modern Museum Initiation	1861 – 1950	1905 – 1936
II	Community Education Platform	1950 – 1969	1949 – 1976
III	Growth with National Reform	1969 – 1989	1978 – 1990
IV	Rethinking Museum Development	1990 – 2000	1990 – 2010
V	Objective Driven Management	2000 –	2011 –

oping countries have integrated the social mission and public services of museums into supporting national lifelong learning and creating innovative state programs. For example, 5,600 museums in Japan are part of the three supporting pillars of the citizen lifelong learning system, which is comprised of museums, citizen halls and libraries. By adopting best practices from the U.S. and European countries, Japan has developed a unique Asian style citizens' development system for the creation of a learning society. This has involved enacting education-related laws such as the Museum Law, Social Education Law, Library Law, and Lifelong Learning Law.

There are so many similarities in the developmental path taken by Chinese museums compared with the international community, particularly Japan. Based on the statistical data released by the China State Administration of Culture and Heritage, the number of museums in China has increased from 24 in 1949 to more than 3,000 in 2010. China must fill a great gap to catch up with other countries by integrating the public service functions of museums to support citizen lifelong learning. China is still far behind in terms of social development of a legal framework, operating mechanism, management system, and talent in museum development.

*** ***

Chapter 2   Challenges & Opportunities in Museum Development

(Extrait)
Défis & Possibilités dans le Développement du Musée: Perspective Historique et Sociologique—La Chine contre le Japon

En 2010, la Chine a dépassé le Japon et a devenu la deuxième plus grande économie du monde par trois décennies d'ouverture politique. Dans la même période, le nombre de musées en Chine a augmenté de 300 en 1978 à 3.000 en 2010. Alors qu'au Japon, le nombre de musées a augmenté de 145 en 1945 à 5.000 en 2003. Les méthodologies historico-comparatives appliquées pour étudier le rôle de service public des musées dans des stades différents de développement économique au Japon et à la Chine peuvent révéler de nouvelles perspectives sur l'impact du développement de la culture par la croissance économique régionale. Par comparaison, cinq caractères principaux du Japon contre la Chine sont comme suit : l'initiation par l'administration par rapport à l'association universitaire conduite, la croissance économique par l'éducation publique par rapport au mouvement politique de masse, la maturité par le développement d'étape importante par rapport à la protection des vestiges culturelles, le mythe par pathologie de musée par rapport à la construction matérielle, la future par la performance de gestion par rapport à la mission sociale. En examinant le plan de voie de l'industrialisation en cinq étapes de Rostow (1960) avec la courbe en S améliorée de Porter (2002), l'innovation serait le facteur dominant de conduire l'avenir dans le 21e siècle. Des études menées par le gouvernement des États-Unis, du Royaume-Uni et de l'Australie ont illustré que les rôles des musées, l'éducation, la culture et l'art, l'innovation, le développement social et économique sont liés. Les connaissances des études sociales auraient un impact sur public à inspirer l'innovation pour le développement social et économique.

(Extracto)
Desafíos y Oportunidades en el Desarrollo del Museo: Una perspectiva histórico-sociológica—China en comparación con Japón

A partir de 2010, China superó a Japón como la segunda economía más grande del mundo tras tres décadas de la política de reforma y apertura. Al mismo tiempo, el número de museos de China aumentó de 300 en 1978 a 3000 en 2010. Mientras que en Japón, el número de museos se incrementó de 145 en 1945 a 5000 en 2003. Las metodologías histórico-comparativas aplicadas al estudio sobre las funciones de los museos de servicio público en las diferentes etapas de desarrollo económico en Japón y China pueden revelar nuevas perspectivas sobre el impacto derivado del desarrollo del museo al crecimiento económico regional. Por comparaciones, las cinco características entre Japon y China son las siguientes: la iniciación por la administración frente a por la sociedad académica, el crecimiento económico mediante la educación pública contra mediante el movimiento político de masas, la madurez por el desarrollo histórico frente a por la protección de la cultura reliquias, el mito por el museo de la patología frente a por el edificio de hardware, y el futuro por la gestión del rendimiento en comparación con la misión social. La innovación será el factor dominante para impulsar el futuro para el siglo XXI mediante el examen de Rostow (1960) en una hoja de ruta de cinco etapas para la industrialización con una mejora de la curva S por Porter (2002). Estudios realizados por el gobierno de los EE.UU., Reino Unido y Australia muestran que los papeles de museos, la educación, la cultura y el arte, la innovación, el desarrollo social y económico están relacionados. El conocimiento de las ciencias sociales tendría un impacto público para inspirar a la innovación para el desarrollo social y económico.

Note
1 : The WORLD BANK. GDP <https://data.worldbank.org/indicator/NY.GDP.MKTP.CD>
2 : CIA (2011). The World Factbook <https://www.cia.gov/library/publications/the-world-factbook/>
3 : The WORLD BANK. GDP <https://data.worldbank.org/indicator/NY.GDP.MKTP.CD>
4 : MEXT(2011).博物館の振興<http://www.mext.go.jp/a_menu/01_1/08052911/1313126.htm>
5 : The data is from government informal publication and news release from the State Administration of CultureHeritage for China. Chinese government agencies have limited official publication. The way they disclose information is through various forms of news release.
6 : ICOM Statutes, Approved in Vienna (Austria) August 24, 2007, p. 2. <http://icom.

museum/fileadmin/user_upload/pdf/Statuts/statutes_eng.pdf>
7 : Travers (2006). Museums and Galleries in Britain: Economic, social and creative impacts, London, National Museum Directors' Conference, p. 6. <http://www.nationalmuseums.org.uk/media/documents/publications/museums_galleries_in_britain_travers_2006.pdf>
8 : ibid., p. 16.
9 : Cutler (2008). Report: Venturous Australia-Building Strength in Innovation, Sydney, Ministry for Innovation, Industry, Science and Research, p. viii. <http://www.innovation.gov.au/Innovation/Policy/Documents/NISReport.pdf>
10 : National Commission on Excellence in Education (1983). *A Nation at Risk,* Washington D.C., the U.S. Department of Education, p. 9. <https://files.eric.ed.gov/fulltext/ED226006.pdf>
11 : ibid., p. 9.
12 : Rostow (1960). *The Stages of Economic Growth: A Non — Communist Manifesto,* Cambridge, Cambridge University Press, p. 4.

References

CIA (2011). The World F6actbook <https://www.cia.gov/library/publications/the-world-factbook/>

Cutler (2008). Report: Venturous Australia-Building Strength in Innovation, Sydney, Ministry for Innovation, Industry, Science and Research <http://www.innovation.gov.au/Innovation/Policy/Documents/NISReport.pdf>

Jan-Yen Huang (2005). From the Age of "Cultural Affairs as Administration" to the Age of "Culture Enterprise for the Public": A Critical Study of the Meaning and Challenge of the Administrative Corporation in National Museums in Taiwan, and Comparison with the Japan Experience, Taipei, *Museology Quarterly*.

National Commission on Excellence in Education (1983), *A Nation at Risk,* Washington D.C., the U.S. Department of Education.

Porter (2002). *The Global Competitiveness Report 2001 — 2002,* New York, Oxford University Press.

Rostow (1960). *The Stages of Economic Growth: A Non — Communist Manifesto,* Cambridge, Cambridge University Press.

Teuchi, Akitoshi (2010). Japanese Education System and Practice, Tokyo, Center for Research on International Cooperation in Educational Development (CRICED), University of Tsukuba.

Travers (2006). Museums and Galleries in Britain: Economic, social and creative impacts, London, National Museum Directors' Conference <http://www.nationalmuseums.org.uk/media/documents/publications/museums_galleries_in_britain_travers_2006.pdf>

Travers and Glaister (2004). Valuing Museums: Impact and Innovation Among National Museums, London, National Museum Directors' Conference <http://www.national

museums.org.uk/media/documents/publications/valuing_museums.pdf>

Wang, L. (2009). "Building Conscience Driven Culture by Regional Heritage - Social Mission of Museums for the 21st Century", Proceeding of ICOM ASPAC TOKYO, 2009.

Wang, W. (2006). "Scientific Outlook: Concept and Practice", Beijing, Central Party School Press.

World Bank (2011). World Development Indicators database <http://siteresources.worldbank.org/DATASTATISTICS/Resources/GDP.pdf>

* The Museology Quarterly is indexed in Taiwan Citation Index - Humanities and Social Sciences (TCIHSS) by the National Central Library.

3
Museum 2.0
An Extended Exhibition in Cyberspace by Social Media

Dippel (2002) described the key drivers of social development: Politics, Economy, Knowledge and Media. As early as 1970, some famous sociologists described future trends. We are between two eras—we are in a transition from an old era, an industrial society, to a new era, an information society. Today, social media, digital mobility, and cloud computing are changing the ways that people think and work. What happened to our museum sector over the last three decades? As museum professionals, are we ready for the social change?

Toffler (1980) adopted a theory of "three waves" of culture and community development. The First Wave is the settled agricultural society which prevailed in much of the world after the Neolithic Revolution, which replaced hunter-gatherer cultures. The Second Wave is Industrial Age society. The Second Wave began in Western Europe with the Industrial Revolution, and subsequently spread across the world. The Third Wave is the post-industrial society. Toffler says that since the late 1950s most countries have been transitioning from a Second Wave society into a Third Wave society. He coined many words to describe it and mentions names invented by others, such as "the Information Age."

What is this change? Is this the biggest change since the Industrial Revolution? The author strongly believes that this is the greatest change ever in human history.

There's no ceiling to this change; no place where it has to end. Our museum colleagues have been actively engaged in exploring how future museums can raise public awareness of this change. According to Dr. Mizushima's Museum 5G theory, we are in the fourth generation and approaching the fifth generation of museum development wherein Museum 1G was conceived as a Collection, Museum 2G was conceived for Conservation, Museum 3G for Exhibition & Education, Museum 4G for Digitization for Input/Output, and Museum 5G as a Converter for Participation.

From current developments in cloud computing and social media, the author believes the age of the sixth generation museum has arrived— Museum 6G as Center for Excellence of Cultural Resources Integration and Management.

Figure 1 illustrates the mission management perspective of 6G museum research. Community-centric is the key for us in working to change future museums! Cultural resource management may take into consideration the influence of social media and museum mission on our social mission to build a harmonious society

Figure 1. Museum 6G Research Dimensions — Mission Management

Figure 2 illustrates the process ownership perspective on 6G museum research. Who will be the process owners of the changes in future museums? Traditional museum curators are the ones who lead major efforts and activities for change and development. But this is no longer true. Social media can influence the public not only regarding what it wants to see in physical and digital museums, but also how the public obtains information and converts it into knowledge.

Chapter 3 Museum 2.0

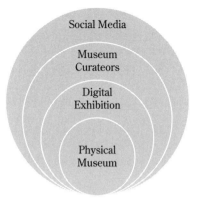

Figure 2. Museum 6G Research Dimensions — Process Ownership

How can museum curators cope with social media? We still have very limited information on the impact of social media on museums. The author used eGov 2.0 as a reference case to study Museum 2.0.

Digitalization has changed the way we work and live. According to the Neilson (2009) report, two-thirds of the world's internet population visits a social network or blogging site, and the sector now accounts for almost 10% of all internet time.

Richardson (2011) created a way to acquire data from the top three social media websites which are Facebook, Twitter, and Klout. By tracking 3,635 museums and galleries, he discovered 11,863,882 "Likes" on Facebook and 12,909,649 Twitter "Followers." Social media is a double-edged sword. Each museum has an average of 8,000 followers who volunteer to pay attention to our daily work not only by voicing their opinions, but by voting to evaluate our work. While water may create a waterway for sailing, water may also sink the ship. Museum professionals must pay special attention to the wide application of social media such as Facebook, Twitter and YouTube. What I call an "extended exhibition" through social media is a new way of influencing society in addition to the traditionally defined permanent or temporary exhibitions.

Are museums and museum professionals ready to surf the wave of information technology in the age of cyberspace? Dicker (2009) conducted a survey entitled, "The Impact of Blogs and Other Social Media on the Life of a Curator" on 96 curators from Australia, the UK, the USA, Norway and New Zealand in 2009. The survey revealed that museum curator roles had been significantly impacted by social media. The traditional roles of a curator as an "expert" or "specialist" are fading away. Researcher or knowledge broker does not truly reflect the reality of the situation today. Social media may generate new voices and new votes which may add new dimensions to the management of extended exhibitions in cyberspace.

Technology development has created new platforms for museums. How will this affect museum curators? Are curators integrating social media into curatorial practice? If so, how are they interacting in these spaces, and what impact does all this have on a curator's role and the collections they care for? Curators are facing challenges in the increased demand for two-way communication, previously the domain of staff working on public programs, outreach, or web editing. Do curators use social media in their personal lives? The majority (80.5%) of all participants surveyed use social media spaces for personal use. The most popular platforms include Facebook, YouTube, Flickr, MySpace, and commenting on blogs. Other uses include LinkedIn, and nings. Curators who have placed themselves in cyberspace for personal use will more likely be part of the networked world of social media. In response to the question, "Curators Who Do Not Use Social Media" in their roles as curators, 36.7% of all survey participants answered that they do not use social media. When asked why, the overwhelming response was that social media takes up time that they just don't have. In fact, 90% of them intoned that they would like more social media training to be offered in their workplace.

You can check your museum's website to see if you are at the Museum 2.0 age. Museum web sites have evolved from the Museum 1.0 or AOL Age which has the following main characteristics: it lets people find your museum by googling, communicate through e-mails and instant messaging, engage in chat rooms while contents are selected by AOL and Yahoo. Considering the Web as a source of information, museum websites were designed to provide

Chapter 3 Museum 2.0

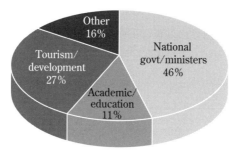

Figure 3. eGoverment 2.0 Application in Asia

information and to plan trips. In the Museum 2.0 or Facebook Age, potential visitors can find your museum through a social network posting. Social media is used as a gateway to the Web. Member communities can have a great influence on society. Their presence on a social network is critical for museums as an effective marketing tool.

The application of Museum 2.0 has many similarities with Government 2.0. Freeman and Loo (2009) suggest there are three categories of benefits that governments can achieve from using Web 2.0 technologies: efficiency, user convenience, and citizen involvement. Museum websites focused on providing museum information, exhibition information, directions and operating hours, and information on planning tours. Government websites focused on policy and information dissemination, education and tourism.

J. Kuzma (2010) examined 50 Asian countries and discovered that only 30% of governments in Asia were using Web 2.0 tools. The rate is much higher in developed countries. Most Asian governments have not realized the importance of social media as an effective tool for communication with its citizens. Lack of strategic direction in utilizing Web 2.0 tools is a common issue. Mixed attitudes toward social media tools including fears and concerns could affect the development of democratic movements. Figure 3 illustrates four categories of usage. Government 2.0 paid extra attention to the censorship of the e-Democracy Movement, fairness for low income families without internet access, sustainability of funding and continuity of operation, and privacy and security protections for citizens. It is interesting to note that if we replaced "government" for "museum," we could easily reach a similar conclusion.

It is a new global trend to view museums as a knowledge source for civilization which focuses on conscience, wisdom and art. The impact of social media has created tremendous challenges for museum educators in the Information Age.

References

Dicker (2009). The Impact of Blogs and Other Social Media on the Life of a Curator <http://www.museumsandtheweb.com/mw2010/papers/dicker/dicker.html#ixzz29dRORoyN>

Dippel (2002). *The Language of Conscience,* Brenham, Texas, Texas Peacemaker Publications, LLC.

Freeman and Loo (2009). "Web 2.0 and E-government at the Municipal Level," 5th International Conference on e-Government 2009, Boston, MA, U.S.A.

Kuzma (2010). "Asian Government Usage of Web 2.0 Social Media," European Journal of ePractice <http://www.etudasportal.gov.hu/download/attachments/7995452/European+Journal+epractice+Volume+9.6.pdf>

Nielson (2009). Global Faces and Network Places: A Nelson Report on Social Networking's New Global Footprints, Nielson Company <http://www.nielsen.com/us/en/insights/reports/2009/Social-Networking-New-Global-Footprint.html>

Richardson (2011). The Top 50 - Museums in Social Media <http://litot.es/museums-in-social-media/>

Toffler (1980). *The Third Wave,* New York, U.S.A., William Morrow and Company.

Wang (2011). "Challenges & Opportunities in Museum Development A Historic-Sociological Perspective: China versus Japan," Proceeding of ICOM CECA Zagreb, Croatia.

4

The Glory and the Dream
Rethinking the Social Mission of Museums in the Era of Cyber Space

In the fall of 2012, I was invited by ICOM ASPAC 2012 Wuhan to give a speech entitled, "Museums in the Age of Cyber Space: Interdisciplinary Dimensions in the Global Village" and by ICOM CECA 2012 Yerevan to give a speech entitled, "Museum 2.0: An Extended Exhibition in Cyber Space by Social Media." The keywords in my speeches "cyber space" and "social media" overwhelmed majority audiences at both of the conferences. After the conferences, I received numerous inquiries relating to the impact of social media on our social mission and the public services of museums which made me think about this more deeply. As an exchange scholar, I have had the opportunity to think out-of-the-box in conducting a historic and sociologic study on our social mission and the public services of museums in Japan through a comparative study with other nations.

4.1 Museum Modernization in Japan

Japan became the second largest economy by GDP in 1968 on the 100th anniversary of the Meiji Ishin (Meiji Restoration). The 1964 Summer Olympics was an international multi-sport event held in Tokyo from October 10 to 24, 1964. It was the first Olympics ever held in Asia. Expo '70 (Japan World Exposition) was a World's Fair held in Suita, Osaka from March 15 to September 13, 1970. The theme of the Expo was "Progress and Harmony for Mankind." This was the first World Expo held in Asia and Japan realized this dream with glory. Japan was the first nation in Asia admitted into the club of industrial nations and became a rising star from Asia. Japan gave rise to mainstay brands with quality and innovativeness.

Japan's initiation into the society of modern museums can be traced back to the period between 1861 through 1951. The key characteristic of this initiative was that it was "Administration-Driven." The Japanese government kicked off the initial establishment of museums nationwide from a need for the administration of national assets, natural resources, products, and information gathering for national policy on foreign trade and industrial development. Thus, museums in Japan were born with the "DNA" for social economic development. In 1936, 320 museums were established including 10 in Korea and 10 in Taiwan.

Depending on the perspective of one's study, the period from 1969 through 1989 can be considered to be the golden age of museum development. With the celebration programs for the 100th anniversary ceremony of the Meiji Ishin (Meiji Restoration), Japan reached its peak in social and economic development. "Local," "Culture," and "Globalization" became themes for local governments to build new museums. Corporate memorial museums and art galleries became another social trend in museum development. Corporate culture became a buzz word in community development. 150 museums were added per year by the central government, local governments and major corporations. The number of museums reached 3,289 in 1977.

4.2 Mega Trends

Naisbitt's (1982) book, "MEGATRENDS: Ten New Directions Transforming Our Lives" was a best-seller in 57 countries selling 14 million copies. He adopted the principle of research that, "the most reliable way to anticipate the future is by understanding the present." He developed real authority from his long-term perspective on how an information society will be different from the prior industrial one. Here are ten mega-trends he projected: (1) Becoming an information society after having been an industrial one; (2) From technology being forced into use, to technology being pulled into use where it is appealing to people; (3) From a predominantly national economy to one in the global marketplace; (4) From short term to long term perspectives; (5) From centralization to decentralization; (6) From getting help through institutions like government to self-help; (7) From representative to participative democracy; (8) From hierarchies to networking; (9) From a northeastern bias to a southwestern one; (10) From seeing things as "either/or" to having more choices. Three decades later, Naisbitt's predictions were proven true.

What is this change? Is this the biggest change since the Industrial Revolution? I strongly believe this is the greatest change ever in history. There's no ceiling to this change, no place where it has to end. Arthur (2011) described the concept of the second economy. With the coming of the Industrial Revolution—roughly from the 1760s, when Watt's steam engine appeared, to around 1850 and beyond—the economy developed a muscular system in the form of machine power. Now it is developing a neural system. Around 1990, computers started to communicate with each other, and all these connections started to occur. The individual machines—servers—are like neurons, and the axons and synapses are the communication pathways and linkages that enable them to be interconnected with each other and to take appropriate action.

In the early 20th century, farm jobs became mechanized and there was less need for farm labor. Some decades later, manufacturing jobs became mechanized and there was less need for factory labor. Now business processes—many in the service sector—are becoming mechanized, requiring fewer people which is exerting systematic downward pressure on jobs.

What can we learn from this lesson? As one of the key growth engines of the 21st Century, the second economy is creating prosperity without creating many job opportunities. Our society is facing a huge challenge of how to distribute instead of producing prosperity. As we traditionally believe, wealth should be associated with jobs. At the time when we phased out agriculture jobs, we created manufacturing jobs. Furthermore, we phased out blue-collar manufacturing jobs with white-collar service jobs. With this digital transformation, this last repository of jobs is shrinking—fewer of us in the future may have white-collar business process jobs—so we are faced with a problem.

I have been trying to learn what Japan did while other industrial nations were transforming from building "muscular system" to developing "neural system" over the last three decades. In building its muscular system, Japan established many primary brands such as Toyota as dominant global players in manufacturing. Even Americans are learning from Toyota not only in terms of technology and innovation, but also from its management system. However, I cannot see how Japan will be as strong as it used to be. Japan used to be the leader in ICT information communication technology. Japan should create its own "Apple" like Korea did with Samsung to compete with America's "Apple." Most recently, the downgrading of Sony and Panasonic's credit rating to near junk status shows how Japan's leadership position in innovation is deteriorating rapidly.

4. 3 New Trends in museum sector

Let's look at what happened to our museum sector. From 1990 to 2000, 200 museums were added by the central government and local governments as well as communities. Japan lost sight of its vision and mission management of museums in the high tide of museum development. This museum pathology made Japanese museum societies aware of what they should do to reform. Public and Private Partnership (PPP) was introduced by "Mécénat" (Patronage) for the support, encouragement, promotion, or financial aid for museum and art development. The public became aware of lifelong learning to prepare them for the 21st century. From 2000, the Japan Museum Management Academy (JMMA) developed a grading system for museum evaluation. Performance management was introduced using the balanced scorecard (BSC) and other methodologies. Digitalization, Dialogue and Communication for social education with citizen and community participation were advocated. With education reform in 2002, an integrated study time initiative was commenced as part of social education for high school students.

However, public and private funding and support to the museum sector is far from adequate. Personally, I believe what Japan's central government did by the end of 19th century could be re-applied today. A national initiative in cultural resources planning and management could bring the social mission and public services of museums in line with future national innovations.

The Australian government recognized the importance of cultural development and innovation. Cutler (2008) made a clear link from culture and art to economic development through his study on innovation. In his report to the Ministry for Innovation, Industry, Science and Research "Venturous Australia: Building Strength in Innovation," Cutler tried to make the point that there was a large gap between the way culture and the arts sees itself and formal innovation frameworks, policy and programs. The 202 page report not only studied other industrial nations, but also paid attention to emerging economies such as China and India. Believing that innovation is one of the key drivers for the 21st century, Cutler pointed out, "This is the innovative spirit we need to nurture in all Australians.[1]"

4.4 Conclusion

How we work and live has changed dramatically due to digitalization. When you travel to a Third-World county like China or India, you will not be surprised to see how popular smart phone usage is, even for a street vendor at a farmer's market. The Jasmine Revolution in Africa and the Mid-East is another example how the Internet may even impact the development of democracy. According to a report by Neilson (2009), two-thirds of the world's Internet population visits a social network or blogging site and the sector now accounts for almost 10% of all time on the Internet.

According to the ICOM Statutes approved in Vienna in 2007, a museum is a non-profit, permanent institution in the service of society and its development, open to the public, which acquires, conserves, researches, communicates and exhibits the tangible and intangible heritage of humanity and its environment for the purposes of education, study and enjoyment.[2]

I am very optimistic about the future of our museum sector. Based on the current development of cloud computing and social media, I believe the age of sixth generation of museum has arrived: Museum 6G as a Center for Excellence of Culture Resources Integration and Management. As a leading nation, I believe Japan can pursue its social responsibility in cooperation with other Asian countries for a regional cultural renaissance and prosperity in the 21st century. Japan built up its powerful "muscular system" in the industrial age such as with Toyota. Japan will rebuild its past glory through Sony/Panasonic to achieve a powerful "neural system" in transitioning to the information age. That should be the mission of our museums and museum professionals in the Asia-Pacific Region.

Note
1 : Cutler (2008). Report: Venturous Australia - Building Strength in Innovation, Sydney, Ministry for Innovation, Industry, Science and Research.
2 : ICOM Statutes, Approved in Vienna (Austria) August 24, 2007, p.2. <http://icom.museum/fileadmin/user_upload/pdf/Statuts/statutes_eng.pdf>

Reference
Arthur (2011). "The Second Economy," McKinsey Quarterly, <http://www.mckinseyquarterly.com/The_second_economy_2853#AboutTheAuhor>
CIA (2011). The World Factbook <https://www.cia.gov/library/publications/the-world-factbook/>
Cutler (2008). Report: Venturous Australia - Building Strength in Innovation, Sydney, Ministry for Innovation, Industry, Science and Research.
Dippel (2002). The Language of Conscience, Brenham, Texas, Texas Peacemaker Publications, LLC.
Naisbitt (1982). Mega Trends: Ten New Directions Transform Our Lives, New York, NY, U.S.A., Grand Central Publishing.
Nielson (2009). "Global Faces and Network Places: A Nelson Report on Social Networking's New Global Footprints," Nielson Company.
Wang (2011). "Challenges & Opportunities in Museum Development A Historic-Sociological Perspective: China versus Japan," Proceeding of ICOM CECA Zagreb, Croatia.
Wang, W. (2006). "Scientific Outlook: Concept and Practice," Beijing, Central Party School Press.
World Bank (2011). World Development Indicators database <http://siteresources.worldbank.org/DATASTATISTICS/Resources/GDP.pdf>

5

Digital Engagement as a Catalyst in Transforming Museums, Libraries and Archives

A Case Study of the Field Museum of Natural History

5.1 Background

Wang (2012) addressed the impact on museums by social media and digitalization. What is this change? Is this the biggest change since the Industrial Revolution? The author believes that this is the greatest change in history. There's no ceiling to this change; no place where it has to end. It's not only that museums, libraries and archives (hereafter, "MLA") are changing how they think about their audiences; it's that their audiences are changing how they think about MLA. The role of MLA is being reimagined from within and without, amounting to an epic shift in expectations. The dedication to art, history, and culture remains, but its social function is different from what it was.

Dippel (2002) described the key drivers of social development: Politics, Economy, Knowledge and Media. As early as 1970, some of the most famous sociologists described future trends—how we are in a transition from an old era, an industrial society, to a new era, an information society. Today, social media, digital mobility, and cloud computing are changing the ways people are accustomed to thinking and working.

Toffler (1980) proposed a theory of "three waves" to describe culture and community development. The First Wave is the settled agricultural society which prevailed in much of the world after the Neolithic Revolution which replaced hunter-gatherer cultures. The Second Wave is Industrial Age society. The Second Wave began in Western Europe with the Industrial Revolution and subsequently spread across the world. The Third Wave is the post-industrial society. Toffler says that since the late 1950s, most countries have been transitioning from a Second Wave society into a Third Wave society. He coined many words to describe it and mentions names invented by others, such as "the Information Age."

The author will address new phenomena in showing how digital engagement may impact the future development and the current operation of MLA. This will be accomplished through a horizontal study of the strategic management of MLA. To obtain baseline information, an integrated approach by MLA into local educational, cultural, and economic systems in the City of Chicago will be studied. A vertical study of the Field Museum's development through innovation from 2006 to 2015 will be pursued.

5. 2 Challenges and Opportunities for MLA

Featuring spectacular artifacts from the tomb of the ancient Egyptian pharaoh, the "Treasures of Tutankhamun" exhibition tour traveled to six cities across the U.S. from 1976 through 1979, and drew millions of people into museums. Americans standing in line for hours to see King Tut marked the advent of a new kind of museum exhibition—the blockbuster. Over a decade ago, MLA leadership had shifted its priorities to community engagement, placing less emphasis on large-scale exhibitions. The cost of a travelling exhibition is prohibitively expensive. A national exhibition tour, perhaps conceivable in the 1980s, is out of the question today.

In the 21st century, visitors will have their own expectations when visiting an MLA institution. They will be interacting with the content on display by curating the virtual exhibits on their own, sharing information about collection items through social media, or participating in public dialog around issues they are interested in. MLA are also realizing that if they want to attract old and new audiences which reflect the diverse communities around them, they need to break down gallery walls.

5. 3 Why The Field Museum

The Field Museum of Natural History in Chicago is one of the largest natural history museums in the world. The museum maintains its status as a pre-

Chapter 5 Digital Engagement as a Catalyst in Transforming Museums, Libraries and Archives

mier natural history museum through the size and quality of its educational and scientific programs. The Field Museum itself is a 3-in-1 MLA facility occupying a building space of 80,000 square meters. Its collection center is host to 24.7 million specimens, with 200,000 items added each year. Its library has 275,000 books, 278 subscriptions to domestic and foreign journals, 1,800 feet of archival records, 7,500 rare books, and 3,000 works of art. Its photo archives consist of 300,000 images. The Field Museum attracts 800–900 visiting professors and research scientists, as well as two million on-site visitors from all continents annually.

The Field Museum

Like most U.S. museums, the Field Museum is a not-for-profit entity supported primarily by private fund raising. It has a well-defined governance structure (board of trustees from local communities) with excellent record keeping. Annual reports are available, dating back to day-one of the museum's commencement in 1983 through to today .

As we all know, less than 1% of collections can be exhibited by a given museum. To build an internet-based infrastructure to provide greater exposure of collections to the public, the Field Museum has put significant resources into upgrading its information technology platform. Here are a few examples. Through its efforts over a ten year period, the Field Museum converted its website into a knowledge source to share its incredible resources with over nine million e-visitors throughout the world on an annual basis as early as 2007. This includes more than 27,500 pages ranging from in-depth teaching guides, to downloadable reference materials for field scientists to use . In 2010, the Field Museum scientists led a project to connect students from Chicago's Austin neighborhood with students in Fiji. This allowed students in Chicago to experience coral reef environments in the Pacific Ocean, to engage in the scientific process, and to participate in real world conservations. The participants consisted of a small group of winners of a grant competition called the 2010 Digital Media and Learning Competition Award that attracted more than 800 applications.[1]

The Field Museum continued allocating its resources to apply advanced technologies to engage visitors. In 2014, the Field Museum upgraded its Internet service to a 1 Gigabit per second (Gbps) Ethernet Dedicated Internet connection with reserved bandwidth to 10 Gbps. The new IT infrastructure gives the Field Museum the bandwidth to support interactive technologies to fulfill visitor needs to explore and engage with its collections, content and exhibits, and to enhance its operations (Segal, 2014).

From internet celebrity to museum scientist, Emily Graslie's story shows how open the Field's leadership is to adopt new forms of communication. Emily was a 20-year-old senior college student majoring in studio art who visited the Field Museum on a whim. Four years later she became the Field's "Chief Curiosity Correspondent" and the host of the Brain Scoop, an educational YouTube channel with more than 200,000 subscribers.

To give visitors a new way to interact with the object without damaging the original, the Museum applied the latest 3-D printing technology to make replicas of historical artifacts. An example of this is a Field Museum exhibition traveling around the country called, "Mummies: New Secrets from the Tombs." A medical CT scanner was used to "unwrap" the mummies. Visitors can peek under the wrappings by manipulating large table-top computer scans placed alongside the delicate specimens to see the clothes, hairstyles and jewelry from the grave.

5.3.1 Mission Statement of the Field Museum

The Field Museum is an educational institution concerned with the diversity and relationships in nature and among cultures. Combining the fields of Anthropology, Botany, Geology, Paleontology, and Zoology, the Field uses an interdisciplinary approach to increasing knowledge about the past, present, and future of the physical earth, its plants, animals, people, and cultures.[2]

5.3.2 The Field Museum Economic Impact Statement

This is a snap shot of the Field Museum's operations in 2011:[3]

- *Undertook more than 60 expeditions, uncovering 200 new plants and animals*
- *Conserved over 1.1 million acres of rainforest in the Amazon's headwaters*
- *Welcomed 1.28 million visitors from every state and over 40 countries*
- *Engaged with over 354,000 children and adults through 1,000 science education programs*
- *Hosted 780 visiting researchers, 53 resident graduate students, and 164 interns*

Figure 1 illustrated how the Field Museum's collection-based research and learning had an economic impact on the local community and generated greater public understanding and appreciation of the world in which we live.

5.4 Digital Engagement

5.4.1 Digital Engagement Driving Social Development

In 2012, the Grainger Foundation gave a special gift to the Field Museum to support its giant leap in digital engagement. The purpose of this grant was to study five initiatives: ***technology infrastructure, digital imaging of collection objects, planning for the Museum's new Digital Learning Lab, digital technologies for exhibits, and the development of new offerings to the audience***. The study covered digital engagement from CT scanners for scientific research to

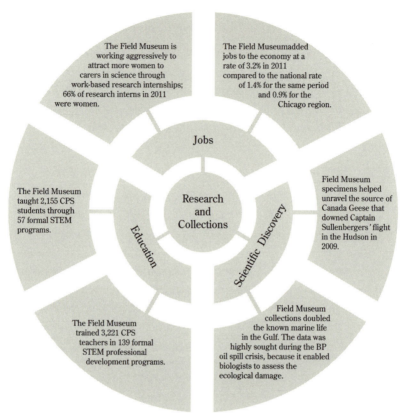

Figure 1. The Field Museum 2011 Economic Impact Statement
Data Source: The Field Museum's Impact to Local community[4]

improvements to the building's Wi-Fi system.

Slover Linett Audience Research Inc. (2014) was engaged to conduct this study for two years. The study went through two phases. The primary aim of Phase 1 is to uncover motivations, preferences, and experiences that museum visitors may be unable to deliberately articulate (Slover Linett Audience Research Inc., 2013a). The key objectives of the Phase 2 survey are: to quantify and measure the prevalence of these motivations, meaning-making priorities, and technological ideals uncovered in exploratory Phase 1 research; and to identify distinct attitudinal segments that exist within the Field's visitor base according to these motivations and ideals to help the museum identify strategies for the incorporation of new technologies in ways that best serve the needs of different visitor segments (Slover Linett Audience Research Inc., 2013b).

How can technology applications fulfill visitor expectations for museum experiences? The study suggests two tracks: by giving them ways to get closer to the museum's content (nature and human cultures); and by giving them a platform for shared experiences and meaning-making with their visiting companions.

5. 4. 2　Changing Visitor Expectations by Segment

The quantitative study confirmed that visitors are generally excited when they are exposed to new digital tools in their visiting experience. Nearly three-quarters of visitors thought that new technologies have the potential to enhance the visiting experience, and two-thirds said they would "love" to see the museum incorporate more such technologies into its exhibitions. In fact, the level of interest in technology was largely independent of demographic factors such as age, education, and income. The study revealed that there were about as many older visitors excited about new technology as younger ones, and about as many young people who saw the museum as an oasis away from high-tech gear as older visitors.

Another key point that can be taken away from the study is that many visitors are already using their own technologies in the museum to capture memories of their experiences, often in highly social and sometimes humorous ways. (About three-quarters report using cameras, smartphones, or tablets to take photos during their museum visits.) A minority are also using their devices to enhance their exhibition experience, for instance by looking up a question or topic of interest during their visit (23%) or looking up this information once they arrive at home (38%).

To cover the museum experience needs of different segments, the Field Museum developed a "layering" approach to strategically mix a variety of digital and technological experiences with more conventional forms of presentation in any given exhibition. The proportion of this mix would depend on the goals, intended audiences of the exhibition, and perhaps the intended sequence and distribution of experiences in the museum as a whole. Table 1

Table 1. Museum Visitor Typology with Motivations, Engagement, and Technology references

Segment	Curious Activity-Seekers	Contemplative Traditionalists	Social Explorers	Parent-Facilitators
Visitor Expectations	32%	24%	18%	16%
What do they want to get out of their Field Museum experience?	Intellectual growth, gaining new knowledge and perspectives, experiencing a top Chicago attraction (most are tourists)	Engaging with particular topics of interest (esp. nature), gaining new knowledge and perspectives	Connecting with loved ones; relaxing and recharging	Providing enriching and educational experiences for their children
How do they prefer to engage with museum content?	Interactive, hands-on, participatory experiences they can enjoy individually	Reading and looking at artifacts, talking with their companions	Talking with their companions, open-ended exploration of ideas and exhibition content	Interactive, hands-on, participatory experiences they can enjoy with their children
How can technology support their desired experience?	Mobile app tours to help them see the "best of" the Field, digital interactives that focus on challenging their assumptions and giving them new perspectives	By not interfering with their experience; consider using mainly handheld or atmospheric technologies in exhibitions where they can commune with nature and human cultures	Interactive displays featuring open-ended exploration of content, games, etc. that serve as a platform for shared meaning- and memory-making	Digital displays featuring games, mini-"science experiments" and other interactive activities alongside more traditional hands-on activities

Source: Slover Linett Audience Research Inc. (2014). What Makes a Great Museum Experience and How Can Technology Help? Visitor Research and Segmentation for The Field Museum's Grainger Initiatives, p. 9[5].

is a good reference tool for this process.

While every exhibition planning team should at least consider the needs of all four of these key segments, that doesn't mean every exhibition must attempt to engage each segment equally; the exhibition team can dial up or down the aspects of the experience that are likely to serve different audiences. The idea is to be intentional and strategic about those decisions in light of what is known about the audience.

5.5 Social Mission of MLA

According to Wang (2009), it is a new global trend to view MLA as a knowledge source for civilization that focuses on conscience, wisdom and art. According to the ICOM Statues adopted in Vienna in 2007, a museum is "a non-profit, permanent institution in the service of society and its development, open to the public, which acquires, conserves, researches, communicates and exhibits the tangible and intangible heritage of humanity and its environment for the purposes of education, study and enjoyment."

The ICOM Statues were initially drafted with an emphasis on collection and conservation, but were soon revised to include preserving, studying and enhancing in 1951. In 2007, education became the top common goal for the fundamental services of museums, over and above "study and enjoyment." The special attention paid toward the public services of museums by the ICOM community reflected its focus on its social mission. It also reflected the important roles the museum sector played in instilling geographic culture and heritage, and fundamental values.

5.6 Awareness of Strategic Positioning of Museums

In the 21st century, the public has more leisure time for enjoyment and to pursue lifelong learning programs for professional development. As museums increasingly focus their attention on audience development and on better serving their visitors, potential audiences are deluged by an increasing volume of information and channels, creating competition for the public's time between leisure and learning opportunities. Thus, growing public participation in museums has brought about the challenge of increased competition. It is becoming an important issue for museum leadership to identify how museums may use strategies of positioning and branding to more effectively target their communication to priority audiences and to position their offerings in a context that is both meaningful and memorable to fulfill the responsibilities of their social mission.

Prevenost (2013) conducted a study for the American Association of Community Theater to help the cultural industry develop a better understanding of branding, positioning and strategic issues. Identity branding is about who you are. Positioning an organization is about where you are. Strategic positioning is about where you want to be in relation to others. Museum leadership needs to understand how to create alignment between its goals and the goals of community development. Museum leadership needs to understand how they want to be recognized in relation to other organizations and then to apply those findings across the board, from program development, donor services, facility planning, season schedules, to special events. Effective positioning may benefit any museum in leveraging its strengths, providing direction in its communications, and reinforcing its case for support in fundraising, development, and organizational advancement efforts.

The following are the mission and vision statements of museums in our case study which clearly reveal how leading museums seek to position themselves:

The Art Institute of Chicago
The Art Institute of Chicago collects, preserves, and interprets works of art of the highest quality, representing the world's diverse artistic traditions, for the inspiration and education of the public and in accordance with our profession's highest ethical standards and practices.

The Museum of Science + Industry
The museum mission is to inspire the inventive genius in everyone. The museum vision is to inspire and motivate our children to achieve their

full potential in science, technology, medicine and engineering.

Kotler (2008) defines positioning as, "the act of designing an organizational Image, values, and offerings so that consumers understand, appreciate, and are drawn to what the organization stands for in relation to its competitors.[7]"

Mosena (2011) made the following statement in his 2010 annual report: "We did it! After six years of careful planning, inspired support and solid execution, the Museum of Science and Industry, Chicago (MSI) completed the mission of our Science Rediscovered capital campaign [19]. Together, we raised $208.8 million—a great accomplishment under tough economic conditions. The Museum now serves as a new model for 21st century science education and programming. And we are very well positioned to pursue our vision to inspire and motivate our children to achieve their full potential in the fields of science, technology, medicine and engineering.[8]" A $208.8 million U.S. dollars raised by one museum from 2004 to 2010, especially in a rather tough economic environment, was clear evidence that the community will support its museums if the right strategic plan is in place.

Let's examine what happened to the local community. According to Chicago's World Business Report, the economy continued to show signs of recovery in 2011. Employment rebounded in education, healthcare, and professional/business services; regional output grew by 3.2 percent; and exports increased by 2 percent from 2010 (chemical and industrial machinery exports grew by more than 25% each). Sales of commercial space and development sites throughout the Chicago region were 83 percent higher in 2011 ($10.8 billion compared to $5.9 billion in 2010). Leading the way was industrial sales which improved from $800 million in 2010 to $2.8 billion in 2011. The Year of 2011 was particularly notable for Chicago area startups which raised more venture capital than in any year since 2001, according to the National Venture Capital Association. Awards received by the City of Chicago:
This is a true story of museums making great strides in aligning their mission with the community they are serving.

5.7 Social Media, Waterway or Flood

Richardson (2011) created a way to acquire data from the top three social media websites—Facebook, Twitter, and Klout. By tracking 3,635 museums and galleries, he identified 11,863,882 "Likes" on Facebook and 12,909,649 Twitter "Followers." Each museum has an average of 8,000 followers who are essentially on duty as volunteers, paying attention to our daily work not only to voice their opinions, but to evaluate our work through their votes. While water may create a waterway for sailing, it may also sink the ship as well. Museum professionals must pay special attention to the wide application of social media such as Facebook, Twitter and YouTube.

Wang (2012) expressed concerns about the effect of process ownership on change in future museums given the strong influence of social media. Traditional museum curators are the ones who led major efforts and activities for change and development. But not anymore! Today, social media can influence what the public wants to see in physical and digital museums, but also how the public obtains information and how it transforms that information into knowledge. Figure 2 illustrates the process ownership perspective of the MLA research dimension. It is interesting that information flow is rather isolated to each layer of business process ownership.

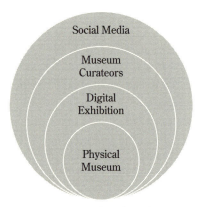

Figure 2. Social Media Influence

Chapter 5 Digital Engagement as a Catalyst in Transforming Museums, Libraries and Archives

Digitalization has changed the ways that we work and live. According to the Neilson (2009) report, two-thirds of the world's Internet population visits a social network or blogging site and this sector now accounts for almost 10% of all internet time usage. Dicker (2009) conducted a survey entitled, "The Impact of Blogs and Other Social Media on the Life of a Curator" targeting 96 curators from Australia, the UK, the USA, Norway and New Zealand. The survey revealed that the museum curator role has been impacted significantly by social media. Social media may generate new voices and new votes which may add new dimensions to the management of extended exhibitions in cyberspace.

Technology development has created a new platform for museums. What will be the impact on museum curators? Are curators integrating social media into curatorial practice? If so, how are they interacting in these spaces, and what impact does all this have on a curator's role and the collections they care for? The Field Museum has created the best business process for information flow by removing the partitions between the layers. It proved how digital engagement is a catalyst in transforming MLA into a knowledge source for social development. Figure 3 illustrates how all the "walls" have been removed. For example, the use of a CT scanner by the Field Museum for "Mummies: New Secrets from the Tombs" removed the clear boundary that existed between the physical and digital exhibition.

Figure 3.   Community Culture Resources Integration

5. 8 Lessons Learned

The case of the Field Museum is not an isolated case. The phenomenon is well rooted in the U.S. political, economic, and cultural soil. In the U.S., there are 123,000 libraries and 17,500 museums. The Institute of Museum and Library Services (IMLS) is a federal government agency which seeks to encourage libraries and museums to advance innovation, lifelong learning, and cultural and civic engagement through grant making, research, policy development and national partnerships.

In the City of Chicago, there are over 100 museums, art galleries and other cultural institutes, and a central library with 80 locations[9]. The National Archives at Chicago house about 10 billion logical data records describing 527,000 artifacts and accounting for 81% of national records. There are also 922,000 digital copies of already digitized materials[10].

The report provides many examples of how we meet our high priority goals: helping museums and libraries offer engaging learning experiences, enabling them to be ***strong community anchors***, aiding in the care of museum and library collections, and promoting ***use of technology to increase access to content***." (IMLS 2013 Annual Report[11]).

The Field Museum, The Museum of Science + Industry, The Art Institute of Chicago, Chicago Central Library, and the National Archives at Chicago are world class institutions. They are leading innovation and change in the MLA sector. A more comprehensive Public-Private Partnership (PPP) model is essential for them in following a well-defined social mission for community development.

Note
1 : It is summary from Field Museum's website and annual reports over last ten years.
   https://www.fieldmuseum.org/about/history
   https://www.fieldmuseum.org/about/annual-reports

Chapter 5　Digital Engagement as a Catalyst in Transforming Museums, Libraries and Archives

2 : Office of Academic Affairs(1997). THE FIELD MUSEUM COLLECTIONS AND RESEARCH FEBRUARY 1997, p.4. <https://www.fieldmuseum.org/sites/default/files/annual_report1997_0.pdf>
3 : The Field Museum Annual Report 2011, p.1. <https://www.fieldmuseum.org/sites/default/files/2011 Annual Report 0.pdf>
4 : The Field Museum's Impact to Local Community <https://www.fieldmuseum.org/sites/default/files/Economic%20Impact%20State ment%20 2011-modified.pdf> Translation of the chart has been updated by a separate file.
5 : Slover Linett Audience Research Inc. (2014). What Makes a Great Museum Experience and How Can Technology Help? Visitor Research and Segmentation for The Field Museum's Grainger Initiatives, p.9. <http://www.slaudienceresearch.com/files/publications/Executive%20summary%20-%20Field%20Museum%20visitor%20experience%20and%20technology%20research%20-%2 0Slover%20Linett.pdf>
6 : ICOM Statutes, Approved in Vienna (Austria) August 24, 2007, p. 2. <http://icom.museum/fileadmin/user_upload/pdf/Statuts/statutes_eng.pdf>
7 : Kotler P. (2008) *Museum Marketing and Strategy: Designing Missions, Building Audiences, Generating Revenue and Resources*, John Wiley & Sons, San Francisco, p.130.
8 : Mosena (2011). Annual Report of Museum of Science and Technology, Chicago <http://www.msichicago.org/join-and-support/leadership/annual-report/>
9 : Chicago Central Library <https://en.wikipedia.org/wiki/Chicago Public Library>
10 : National Archives at Chicago <https://www.archives.gov/chicago>
11 : IMLS 2013 Annual Report, p.1. <https://www.imls.gov/publications/2013-annualreport>

*IMLS Institute of Museum and Library Services is a federal government agency in the U.S. The agency is funded through the U.S. Congress.

Reference
Chicago Central Library <https://en.wikipedia.org/wiki/Chicago Public Library>
Chicago World Business Report 2011 <https://www.dropbox.com/s/4qrpwddycjdtkw8/WBC-2011-Annual-Report.pdf?dl=0>
Dicker (2009). "The Impact of Blogs and Other Social Media on the Life of a Curator", <http://www.museumsandtheweb.com/mw2010/papers/dicker/dicker.html#ixzz29dRORoy N>
Dippel (2002). The Language of Conscience, Brenham, Texas, Texas Peacemaker Publications, LLC., pp.22-102.
Field Museum technology project wins prestigious award <https://www.eurekalert.org/pub releases/2010-05/fm-fmt051010.php>
How Emily Graslie went from YouTube science star to full-time at the Field Museum <http://www.chicagoreader.com/chicago/field-museum-emily-graslie-brain-scoop-

youtube/Content?oid= 12236428>
IMLS 2013 Annual Report <https://www.imls.gov/publications/2013-annual-report>
Kotler P. (2008). Principles of Marketing, New York, *Pearson Prentice* Hall, pp.281-348.
List of Museums and Cultural Institutes in Chicago <https://en.wikipedia.org/wiki/List of museums and cultural institutions in Chicago>
Mosena (2011).Annual Report of Museum of Science and Technology, Chicago <http://www.msichicago.org/join-and-support/leadership/annual-report/>
Museum Visitor Typology with Motivations, Engagement, and Technology Preferences <http://www.slaudienceresearch.com/files/publications/Executive%20summary%20-%20Field%20Museum%20visitor%20experience%20and%20technology%20research%20-%20Slover%20Linett.pdf>
National Archives at Chicago <https://www.archives.gov/chicago>
Nielson (2009). "Global Faces and Network Places: A Nielson Report on Social Networking's New Global Footprints," Nielson Company.
Prevenost (2013). Beyond Branding: Strategic Market Positioning, ARTS INSIGHTS - MARCH 2013.
Richardson (2011). "The Top 50 - Museums in Social Media" <http://litot.es/museums-in-social-media>
Segal, Jack (2014). "The Field Museum in Chicago Uses Advanced Technologies to Engage Visitors," Market Wired <http://www.marketwired.com/press-release/the-field-museum-in-chicagouses-advanced-technologies-to-engage-visitors-nasdaq-cmcsa-1899383.htm>
Slover Linett Audience Research Inc. (2013a). Field Museum • Grainger Initiatives, May 17, 2013, Phase 1: Exploratory Qualitative Research Report of Key Findings and Recommendations <http://www.slaudienceresearch.com/files/publications/Phase%201%20qualitative%20report%20-%20Field%20Museum%20Grainger%20research%20-%20Slover%20Linett.pdf>
Slover Linett Audience Research Inc. (2013b). Field Museum • Grainger Initiatives December 12, 2013, Phase 2: Visitor Survey and Segmentation Report of Key Findings and Recommendations <http://www.slaudienceresearch.com/files/publications/Phase%202%20survey%20and%20segmentation%20report%20-%20Field%20Museum%20Grainger%20research%20-%2 0Slover%20Linett.pdf>
Slover Linett Audience Research Inc. (2014). What Makes a Great Museum Experience and How Can Technology Help? Visitor Research and Segmentation for The Field Museum's Grainger Initiatives
<http://www.slaudienceresearch.com/files/publications/Executive%20summary%20-%20Field%20Museum%20visitor%20experience%20and%20technology%20research%20-%2 0Slover%20Linett.pdf>
The Field Museum 2007 Annual Report <https://www.fieldmuseum.org/sites/default/files/2007 Annual Report.pdf>
The Field Museum Annual Report 2011 <https://www.fieldmuseum.org/sites/default/

files/2011 Annual Report 0.pdf>
The Field Museum's Impact to Local Community <https://www.fieldmuseum.org/sites/default/files/Economic%20Impact%20State ment%20 2011-modified.pdf>
Toffler (1980). *The Third Wave*, New York, U.S.A., William Morrow and Company, pp.32-112.
Wang L. (2012). Museum 2.0 - An Extended Exhibition in the Cyber Space by Social Media, Proceeding of ICOM CECA, Yerevan, Armenia.
Wang, L. (2009). "Building Conscience Driven Culture by Regional Heritage – Social Mission of Museums for the 21st Century," Proceeding of ICOM ASPAC TOKYO, 2009.

*All above websites were accessed from January 1 through March 31, 2017.

6

Empowerment of Citizens with Informatics
Museums, Libraries and Archives in Cyberspace

6.1 2nd economy and social development

Over the last three decades, the extensive developments and innovations in cyberspace are transforming how we live, work and think. For example, "smart" devices, such as the iPhone and iPad, have facilitated the retrieval and sharing of information before, during, and after public visits to an MLA (Museum, Library, and Archive) location. MLA are in the public eye without being restricted by the confines of culture, heritage or language in our global village by way of social networks on the Internet. According to Statista Portal (2017), six billion users are on the top five social media networks.

A wave of informal learning in cyberspace is reshaping our formal education. MLA professionals have become more proactive in rethinking exhibition design criteria, education curriculum development, information technology application, human capital development, and public advocacy initiatives.

Lessons can be drawn from the history of adult education for community development. Effective case studies will help us face challenges in dealing

Table 1. Top 5 social media networks

social media	Users (millions)
Facebook	1,968
WhatsApp	1,200
YouTube	1,000
Face book Messenger	1,000
WeChat	889

Data Source: Statista Portal (2017)[1]

with the wave of information technology.

Studies on the strategic positioning of MLA are becoming popular tools to pursue best practices in citizen empowerment using informatics. Future trend analysis of MLA strategic development in the information age must be considered to position the social mission of MLA in the 21st century.

Both old school and new school rules should be addressed for strategic management. Tapscott (2010) pointed out that the new economy exists concurrently with social development in the information age . Today, the gaming of rules has not changed fundamentally, while capitalism still works as in the context of a free-market system. However, the characteristics of 21st century capitalism has shaped a new economy entirely different from the old economy. Tapscott's famous "Six Reasons There is a New Economy[2]" is explained below:

1. New infrastructure for wealth creation. Networks, specifically the internet, are becoming the basis of economic activity and progress. Unlike how railroads, roads, the power grid, and the telephone supported the vertically integrated business, horizontal and vertical integration would keep changing our community into an all new eco system.
2. New business models. Instead of thinking of New Economy companies as internet technology-based companies or dot-coms e-commerce based companies,
3. New sources of value. In our knowledge-based economy today, value is created by brain power.
4. New ownership of wealth. In the old days of industrial capitalism, the silk- hatted tycoons owned most of the wealth. Today, 60 percent of Americans have assets in the financial market, and the biggest shareholders are labor pension funds.
5. New education models and institutions. The post-industrial revolution era generated much greater demand for lifelong learning. The model of pedagogy is also changing with the growth of interactive, self-paced, student-focused learning.
6. New governance. Cloud computing with big data will further break down silos of government agencies for greater efficiency. A horizontal rather than vertical governance structure will transform an administrative gov-

ernment into a service-oriented government.

The popularity of Web 2.0 was acknowledged in TIME magazine's Person of The Year 2006 issue. In the cover story, Lev Grossman explains, "It's a story about community and collaboration on a scale never seen before. It's about the cosmic compendium of knowledge Wikipedia and the million-channel people's network YouTube and the online metropolis MySpace. It's about the many wresting power from the few and helping one another for nothing and how that will not only change the world but also change the way the world changes.[3]"

6.2 Rethinking the social mission and public services of museums

6.2.1 Social mission

According to Wang (2009), it is a new global trend to view MLA as a knowledge source for civilization with focus on conscience, wisdom and art. According to the ICOM Statues adopted in Vienna in 2007, a museum "is a non-profit, permanent institution in the service of society and its development, open to the public, which acquires, conserves, researches, communicates and exhibits the tangible and intangible heritage of humanity and its environment for the purposes of education, study and enjoyment." The theme of ICOM ASPAC 2009 was "Rethinking the Core Value of a Museum and Regional Heritage in Asia-Pacific." The theme of ICOM 2010 was "Museums and Harmonious Society.[4]"

6.2.2 Global practice in the public services of museums

Over the last three decades, many countries have integrated the social mission and public services of museums into the areas of supporting national lifelong learning and creating innovative state programs. For example, almost 6,000 museums in Japan comprise the three supporting pillars of the citizen lifelong learning system, which includes museums, public halls and libraries. On the other hand, the U.S. is home to 123,000 libraries and 17,500 museums. The purpose of the Institute of Museum and Library Services is to help these institutions provide exemplary public service to millions of lifelong learners

(IMLS, 2013). We need to assist the public in transforming their perception to make MLA their lifelong learning platform. The first-line educator at an MLA should become a "knowledge broker." The entire life-cycle of knowledge brokering should be provided to the public—from creating, acquiring, assimilating, using, to disseminating.

Current developments in the cultural sector will generate more opportunities and challenges for MLA. Over time, new business sectors will likely be generated, while at the same time, make certain businesses obsolete. Information and communication technology (ICT) is driving the creation of a quaternary sector of industry in the 21st century. We have named this period the information or knowledge era.

We classify movies, publishing, music, drama, opera, and the media-related industry as cultural industries. How should we position the MLA sector? Massive data communication by MLA could be viewed as a key driver of the cultural industry, or the core business of MLA.

6.3 Challenges in cyberspace

6.3.1 Member communities

Digitalization has changed how we work and live. According to the Neilson report, two-thirds of the world's internet population visit a social network or blogging site, and this sector now accounts for almost 10% of all internet time (NIELSEN, 2009).

6.3.2 Impact of social media on creating new roles for museum curators

Are museums and museum professionals ready to surf the wave of information technology in the age of cyberspace? Dicker conducted a survey which revealed that museum curator roles were significantly impacted by social media. The traditional roles of the curator as "expert" or "specialist" are fading away (DICKER, 2010).

"Researcher" or "knowledge broker" does not truly reflect the reality of a curator today. Social media may generate new voices and new votes which may add new dimensions for the management of extended exhibitions in cyberspace.

Technology development has created new platforms for museums. How will this impact museum curators? Are curators integrating social media into curatorial practice? If so, how are they interacting in these spaces, and what impact does all this have on a curator's role and the collections which they care for? Curators are facing challenges from an increased demand for bilateral or even multi-lateral communication, previously the domain of staff working on public programs, outreach, or web editing.

6.3.3 Museum website evolution: Web 1.0 to 2.0

The following four points are generally considered the main characteristics of Web 2.0:

1. Information Sharing (1 to 1, 1 to many, many to 1, and many to many)
2. Interoperability (ability of diverse systems and organizations to seamlessly work in concert)
3. User-friendly design (user-centric philosophy)
4. Collaboration (multiple parties working together for a common goal)

Museum website evolution has been impacted by the rapid development of social media, which is considered the gateway to our cyber space. The early state of social media was labeled the AOL Age and the Web was used simply as a source for information. Museum websites were designed to provide information and support trip planning.

Now in the Facebook Age, potential visitors can find a museum by its social network posting. Social media has become the gateway to the Web and the strong influence of member communities will seriously challenge the roles of museum authorities. The presence of museum curators on a social network should be considered an administrative role.

6.4 MLA strategic management

6.4.1 Awareness of the strategic positioning of MLA

In the 21st century, the public has more leisure time to enjoy life and engage in lifelong learning programs for their professional development. As MLA increasingly focus their attention on audience development and better service to visitors, their potential audience is deluged by an increasing volume and channels of information that offer choice between leisure and learning opportunities. Thus, growing public participation in MLA is being challenged by greater competition.

It is of growing importance for museum leaders to identify how MLA use positioning and branding strategies to more effectively target their priority audiences. MLA need to position their offerings in a context that is both meaningful and memorable in order to fulfill their responsibilities based on their social mission.

6.4.2 Setting strategies for MLA

Porter (2007) further elaborated his theory on competitive strategies for the museum sector. He pointed out that an organization may promote the public good, but serving the community through charity, philanthropy, and giving are components of the wrong mindset. Rather, the right goals include delivering social services, meeting the needs of a "customer," and achieving high value.

Doing good requires good strategy. The most important step is to define appropriate goals, which will then guide the MLA operation in answering critical questions—where to serve, what services to provide, how to serve, and how to align these services with the community's developmental goals. The obligation of the MLA is to create social value in such a way as to minimize the resources engaged while maximizing social benefits. Defining, measuring and reporting are the three fundamental steps to implement any strategic initiative.

Below are the top three conceptually-flawed past ways of thinking[5]:

1. "*Strategy as aspiration*: Our strategy is to serve one thousand families and create 250 jobs..."
2. "*Strategy as action*: Our strategy is to erect a new building and ... give $100,000 in family support."
3. "*Strategy as vision /mission*: Our strategy is to serve our community and ... to demonstrate our charity."

Strategy is an overall approach to creating maximum social value for the target recipients/customers. Setting goals for the social services of a museum requires specifying and weighing the social benefits to be achieved. In practice, goal definition and strategy are inextricably intertwined for museums as nonprofit organizations.

6. 5 MLA and 21st century skills: IMLS initiative in the U.S.A.

6. 5. 1 What the internet brought to us

The wide deployment of cloud-based technologies delivered over utility networks has contributed to the rapid growth of online videos and rich media. Our current expectations are that the data network will have almost infinite capacity and will be almost cost free. The application of the internet as a catalyst has been constantly challenging us to rethink not only education, but also informal learning.

That Used to be Us: How America Fell Behind in the World It Invented and How We Can Come Back, a book written by Thomas Friedman and Michael Mandelbaum (2011), addresses four major problems America faces today and their solutions. These problems are: globalization, the revolution in information technology, the nation's chronic deficits, and its pattern of energy consumption. These visionary authors describe our new learning ecosystem and why 21st century skills will become critical in these new environments: "For us to grow, we have to educate people to do jobs that don't yet exist, which means we have to invent them and train people to do them at the same time. That is harder, and it is why we need everyone to aspire to be a creative creator or creative server.[5]"

6. 5. 2 How 21st century skills initiative developed

The Partnership for 21st Century Skills ("P21") was formed in 2002 through the efforts of public-private partnership. P21's mission is to serve as a catalyst to spur 21st century readiness in U.S. K12 education by building collaborative partnerships among education, business, communities, and government leaders.

To develop a globally competitive workforce for the future, the P21 initiative identifies the 3Rs and 4Cs as core elements to successfully align the U.S. classroom environment with the real world environment. The 3Rs (Reading, Writing and Arithmetic) include: English, reading or language arts; mathematics; science; foreign languages; civics; government; economics; arts; history; and geography. The 4Cs include: critical thinking and problem solving; communication and collaboration; and creativity and innovation.

While the 3Rs serve as an umbrella for other subjects and core content, the 4Cs are a shorthand for all the skills needed for success in college, in your career, and in life. In Figure 1, the rainbow framework for P21 students shows specific skills, knowledge content, expertise and literacies blended with innovative support systems to help students master the multi-dimensional abilities required of them in the 21st century.

6.5.3　Why IMLS implemented 21st century skills initiative

As a federal government agency, the Institute of Museum and Library Services (IMLS) seeks to encourage libraries and museums to pursue innovation, lifelong learning, and cultural and civic engagement through grant-making, research, policy development and national partnerships. "Success in today's society requires information literacy, a spirit of self-reliance, and a

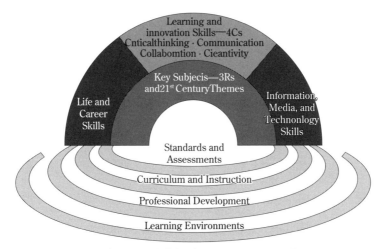

Figure 1.　21st century skill development outcomes and resources
Source: Framework of P21 Skills[7].

strong ability to collaborate, communicate effectively, and solve problems. Combining strengths in traditional learning with robust investment in modern communication infrastructures, libraries and museums are well-equipped to build the skills Americans need in the 21st century".[8]

In light of 21st century demands, libraries and museums should build on their current strengths and embrace new approaches, such as the ones described in Table 2.

Table 2. 21st Museum Library and Archive Transformation

20th Century Museum/Library	21st Century Museum/Library
Primarily content driven	Combination of audience and content driven
Mostly tangible objects	Tangible and digital objects
One-way	Multi-directional
Focus on presentation and display	Focus on audience engagement, experiences
Acts independently	Acts in highly collaborative partnerships
Located in community	Embedded in community
Learning outcomes assumed, implied	Learning outcomes purposeful

Source: IMLS(2008). Museums, Libraries and 21st Century Skills. Washington, DC: Institute of Museum and Library Services IMLS, p. 7.[9]

6. 6 Lessons learned

As a Public-Private Partnership (3P) program, P21 has since 2002 successfully developed a 360 degree framework to build the future workforce. IMLS, the U.S. federal agency which supports museums and libraries in education and public engagement, has lead the MLA sector in participating in the P21 program by immediately piggybacking its guideline on this program. After a decade of development, the U.S. is leading the world economy through innovation. The P21 program has played a great role in social and economic development.

Another author has written on this education-focused initiative in the U.S., which was initiated through the report, "A Nation at Risk" (1983)

A Nation at Risk: *The Imperative for Educational Reform* is a report of American President Ronald Reagan's National Commission on Excellence in

Education. The report pointed out that the U.S., which was once unchallenged in its preeminence in commerce, industry, science, and technological innovation, is at risk of being overtaken by competitors throughout the world. The report referenced Paul Copperman who said that each generation of Americans has outstripped its parents in education, literacy, and economic attainment, but that for the first time in U.S. history, the educational skills of one generation will not surpass, will not equal, and will not even approach those of its parents.

The people of the U.S. need to know that those who do not possess the level of skill, literacy, and training essential to this new era will be effectively disenfranchised, not simply from the material rewards that accompany competent performance, but from the chance to participate fully in the nation's life. A high-level of shared education is essential to a free, democratic society and to the fostering of a common culture, especially in a country that prides itself on pluralism and individual freedom.

Knowledge, learning, information, and skilled intelligence are the new raw materials of international commerce, and are today spreading throughout the world as vigorously as miracle drugs, synthetic fertilizers, and blue jeans did earlier.

The report defined "Five New Basics in the High School Curriculum:" 1) English; 2) mathematics; 3) science; 4) social studies; and 5) computer science. For the college-bound, two years of a foreign language in high school are strongly recommended in addition to those taken earlier.

Based on the five basic subjects for high school learning described in "Our Nation At Risk" (1983) and through the "Partnership for 21st Century Skills in 3R and 4C" since 2002, the U.S. MLA sector has played an important role as an informal learning ecosystem serving the public.

In closing, the Code of Ethics for Museums of the American Association of Museums may provide good perspective on our social mission:

Taken as a whole, museum collections and exhibition materials represent the world's natural and cultural common wealth. As stewards of that wealth, museums are compelled to advance an understanding of all natural forms and of the human experience. It is incumbent on museums to be resources for humankind and in all their activities to foster an informed appreciation of the rich and diverse world we have inherited.[10]

Note
1 : Statista(2017). Social Media Top 5 Social Media Networks Account for 6 Billion Users in 2017 <https://www.statista.com/statistics/272014/global-social-networks-ranked-by-number-of-users/>
2 : TAPSCOTT, Don(2010). "Rethinking in a Netw or why Michael Porter is wrong about Internet," *Strategy + Bussiness*, issue 24, p.5.
3 : You - Yes, You - Are TIME's Person of the Year. <http://content.time.com/time/magazine/article/0,9171,1570810,00.html>
4 : ICOM Statutes, Approved in Vienna (Austria) August 24, 2007, p. 2. <http://icom.museum/fileadmin/user_upload/pdf/Statuts/statutes_eng.pdf>
5 : PORTER, Michael (2007). Doing Well at Doing Good: Do You Have a Strategy? Willow Creek Association Leadership Summit South Barrington, Illinois, August 10, 2007 <http://www.hbs.edu/faculty/Pages/item.aspx?num=46838>
6 : ibid, p.137.
7 : Framework of P21 Skills <http://www.p21.org/about-us/p21-framework>
8 : IMLS(2008). Museums, Libraries and 21st Century Skills. Washington, DC: Institute of Museum and Library Services IMLS <https://www.imls.gov/assets/1/AssetManager/21stCenturySkills.pdf>
9 : ibid., p.7.
10 : AAM. Code of Ethics for Museums. Arlington VA, U.S.A.: American Alliance of Museums, 2000 <http://aam-us.org/resources/ethics-standards-and-best-practices/code-of-ethics>

Reference
AAM. Code of Ethics for Museums. Arlington VA, U.S.A.: American Alliance of Museums, 2000. <http://aam-us.org/resources/ethics-standards-and-best- practices/code-of-ethics>

DICKER, Erika (2010). The Impact of Blogs and Other Social Media on the Life of a Curator, Museums and the Web 2010 - the international conference for culture and heritage on¬line, Denver, Colorado, USA, April 13-17. <http://www.museumsandtheweb.com/mw2010/papers/dicker/dicker.html#ixzz29dROR oyN>

Framework of P21 Skills <http://www.p21.org/about-us/p21-framework>

FRIEDMAN, Thomas and MANDELBAUM, Michael (2011). *That Used to Be Us: How America Fell Behind in the World It Invented and How We Can Come Back*. New York, U.S.A.: Farrar, Straus and Giroux.

IMLS (2008). Museums, Libraries and 21st Century Skills. Washington, DC: Institute of Museum and Library Services IMLS <https://www.imls.gov/assets/1/AssetMana

ger/21stCenturySkills.pdf>

IMLS (2013). Annual Report Number of Museums and Libraries, Washington <https://www.imlsProceeedings....gov/sites/default/files/publications/documents/2013annualreport_0.pdf>

National Commission on Excellence in Education (1983). A Nation at Risk, Washington D.C., the U.S. Department of Education <https://files.eric.ed.gov/fulltext/ED226006.pdf>

Nielson (2009). Global Faces and Network Places: A Nelson Report on Social Networking's New Global Footprints, Nielson Company <http://www.nielsen.com/us/en/insights/reports/2009/Social-Networking-New-Global-Footprint.html>

PORTER, Michael (2007). Doing Well at Doing Good: Do You Have a Strategy? Willow Creek Association Leadership Summit South Barrington, Illinois, August 10, 2007 <http://www.hbs.edu/faculty/Pages/item.aspx?num=46838>

Statista (2017). Social Media Top 5 Social Media Networks Account for 6 Billion Users in 2017 <https://www.statista.com/statistics/272014/global-social-networks-ranked-by-number-of-users/>

TAPSCOTT, Don (2010). Rethinking in a Netw or why Michael Porter is wrong about Internet, *Strategy + Bussiness*, issue 24, p.1-8. <https://faculty.darden.virginia.edu/ebusiness/Tapscott%20Article.pdf>

Wang, L. (2009). "Building Conscience Driven Culture by Regional Heritage – Social Mission of Museums for the 21st Century," Proceeding of ICOM ASPAC TOKYO, 2009.

Epilogue

Turning Information into Intelligence Turing Intelligence into Wisdom

By the end of compiling transcripts of this book, I began to get frustrated as I could not cover as much as I originally envisioned. What am I trying to say? Knowledge, lifelong learning, public empowerment, the third industrial revolution, science, philosophy and religion are all key words which stimulate my thinking. As Albert Einstein said: "Science without religion is lame, religion without science is blind." There is a fine line between being lame and being blind. However, this is just my beginning of authoring books. My writing journey has just begun. I appreciate all readers of this book, and value your collective encouragement and support as I pursue my exploration in searching how best to turn information into intelligence, and turn intelligence into wisdom.

I do believe destiny exists in our world. I think my own destiny is associated with the Tsukuba Mountain. My first trip to the mountain was in 2009 when I first presented at an international conference during ICOM ASPAC Tokyo. Since then, I have been traveling and living in "twin cities": the City of Chicago and the City of Tsukuba. Pursuing my vocation in the museum sector and community development in both North America and Asia has given me unique occidental and oriental perspectives as I search for the best university for my doctoral program. I am using my contribution to the 2017 Catalogue of School of Library, Information and Media, University of Tsukuba as my closing statement.

Right Program, Right University and Right Place

I love our Graduate School of Library, Information and Media Studies for its frontier exploration in turning information into intelligence. As we all learned, the third Industrial revolution is also generating a great impact on our traditional way of learning. The structure setup of our school favors interdisciplinary teaching and multicultural studies. The school's leadership and faculty members are experimenting with transformation from autonomous disciplines with well-defined academic borders, to collaborative networks whose participants come from various fields. At the era of big data, the traditional methodology to the study of phenomena is beginning to give way to the systematic pursuit of big picture issues about the nature of reality and the meaning of existence. My PhD dissertation is focused on Empowerment of Citizens with Informatics–Transformation Trend of Museums, Libraries and Archives for Social Development in the Information Age.

I love the University of Tsukuba for its foremost mission, which is to provide an environment that educates future global leaders to realize their potential in full. Our university gives us the opportunity develop our individuality and skills through an education that is backed by cutting-edge research throughout the world. Our university's various global leadership programs provide the talent and insight for us to successfully navigate humanity through developments, which have been collectively focused around the phenomenon of globalization.

I love the Science City of Tsukuba for its spirit of innovation. The regional concentration of scientific research institutes allows us to promote collaboration among industry, academia and government, and actively contribute to society while continuing to strengthen our education and research capacity. Over the past several decades, Tsukuba has become one of the world's key sites for government-industry collaborations in basic research. The City of Tsukuba has been nicknamed the Second Silicon Valley.

The key drivers of social development consist of Politics, Economy, Knowledge and Media. We are in a transition from an old era; an industrial society, to a new era; an information society. Today, social media, digital mobility, cloud computing and big data are changing the very ways people work and even think. I appreciate this great opportunity to complete the highest academic program of my life at our school. I feel deeply blessed for my truly rich experience at the University of Tsukuba.

Wang Li
Feb. 2018

索引

あ行
IMLS　73
イノベーション　22
異文化コミュニケーション　19
Web 2.0　68
Web 2.0の主な特徴　70
エンパワーメント　66

か行
学習成果　75
学術団体主導　28
拡張展示　37
ガバナンス体制　51
ガバメント2.0　39
官民パートナーシップ　21
企業の記念博物館　29
キュレーションの実践　61
行政主導　43
筋肉系　45
クラウドコンピューティング　68
クラウドベースの技術　73
グローバリゼーション　19
好奇心の通信局長（Chief Curiosity Correspondent）　52

さ行
再生　26
サイバー空間　35
持続可能な発展　23
社会サービス　72
社会的使命　18
巡回展示　50
生涯学習　31
常設展　37
情報科学　66
情報通信技術（ICT）　45
触媒　49
神経系　45
人材開発　67
人文科学　27
人類の進歩と調和　42
3D印刷技術　52
政治宣伝　29
世界最高レベルのベストプラクティス　31
セグメント　55
専門的能力の発展　57
戦略計画　59
戦略的位置づけ　57
戦略的マネジメント　67
創造的刺激を与え教育する　58
ソーシャルメディア　35

た行
第6世代の博物館　36
第三次産業と第四次産業　27
多元主義と個人の自由　76
地域文化の復興　47
知識仲介　20
知識仲介のあらゆる段階　69
知識の源　51
デジタルエンゲージメント　49
デジタル社会への移行　44

展示体験　55

な行
ナレッジベースの経済　67
21世紀型スキル　73

は行
博物館の病　30
非公式学習の生態系　76
ビジョンとミッション管理　45
ビッグデータ　68
フィールド自然史博物館　51
プロセスオーナーシップ　36
文化のリソースの統合　61
文明　25
分野の組み合わせ　52

ま行
ミュージアム1.0　39
ミュージアム2.0　35
明治維新　42
メガトレンド　43
目的主導型　30

ら行
来館者の期待　55
来館者の類型学　56
利用者の発展　57
良知　18
臨時展　37
歴史社会学的方法論　28
歴史的・社会的見地　22
レジャーや学習の機会　71

Index

A Academic Society-Driven 101
Administration-Driven 116
audience development 129
B big data 139
C Catalyst 121
characteristics of Web 2.0 142
Chief Curiosity Correspondent 124
civilization 98
cloud computing 139
cloud-based technologies 144
Conscience 91
Corporate memorial museums 102
cross-cultural communication 92
cultural renaissance 119
Culture Resources Integration 133
curatorial practice 133
Cyberspace 109
D Digital Engagement 121
digital transformation 117
E Empowerment 138
exhibition experience 127
extended exhibition 111
F Field Museum 122
G globalization 92
governance structure 123
Government 2.0 113
H historic-sociological methodology 100
Historic-Sociological Perspective 95
human capital development 138
humanities 100
I ICT information communication technology 118
IMLS 144
informal learning ecosystem 147

Informatics 138
Innovation 95
inspiration and education 130
interdisciplinary 125
K knowledge brokering 93
knowledge source 124
knowledge-based economy 139
L Learning outcomes 146
leisure and learning opportunities 143
life-cycle of knowledge brokering 141
lifelong learning 104
M Mega Trends 116
Meiji Ishin 115
muscular system 117
Museum 1.0 112
Museum 2.0 109
Museum 6G 110
N neural system 117
O Objective Driven 103
P pathology of museums 102
permanent exhibitions 111
pluralism and individual freedom 147
Political propaganda 101
process ownership 110
professional development 129
Progress and Harmony fo Mankind 115
public-private partnership 94
R regeneration 99
S Segment 127
Social Media 109
Social Mission 91
social services 143
strategic management 139
strategic plan 131
Strategic Positioning 129
sustainable development 96
T temporary exhibitions 111

Index

tertiary and quaternary industries 100
3-D printing 124
travelling exhibition 122
21st century skills 144

V vision and mission management 118

Visitor Expectations 127
Visitor Typology 128

W Web 2.0 140
world-class best practice 103

［著者プロフィール］

王　莉（わん・り）
中国の博物館に 6 年間勤務した後，コミュニティ振興学で修士号取得。アメリカの非営利機関に 2 年間勤務。現在，筑波大学大学院図書館情報メディア研究科博士後期課程に在籍。国際博物館会議（ICOM）・教育と文化活動委員会（CECA）会員。日本ミュージアム・マネージメント学会会員。アメリカ・シカゴ市在住。

Wang Li
After working in a famous Chinese Museum for six years, Ms. Wang went to a graduate school for her master degree in community development. Then she worked in a non-profit organization in the U.S. for two more years. Now she is about completing her PhD degree plan in the program of Library, Information and Media Studies in the University of Tsukuba Japan. She is a member of ICOM — CECA (International Council of Museums, Committee of Education and Culture Action). She is also a member of JMMA (Japan Museum Management Academy). She lives in the City of Chicago with her family now.

シリーズ　記録遺産学論考

市民のエンパワーメント
21世紀における博物館・図書館の機能と社会的使命

2018年 2 月22日　初版第 1 刷発行

　　　　　　　　　　　　著　者ⓒ　王　　　　莉
　　　　　　　　　　　　発 行 者　大 塚 栄 一
　　検印廃止
　　　　　　　　　　　　発 行 所　株式会社　樹村房
　　　　　　　　　　　　　　　　　　　　　JUSONBO
　　　　　　　　　　　　〒112-0002
　　　　　　　　　　　　東京都文京区小石川5-11-7
　　　　　　　　　　　　電　話　　03-3868-7321
　　　　　　　　　　　　ＦＡＸ　　03-6801-5202
　　　　　　　　　　　　振　替　　00190-3-93169
　　　　　　　　　　　　http://www.jusonbo.co.jp/

組版・印刷・製本／美研プリンティング株式会社

ISBN978-4-88367-298-1　　乱丁本は小社にてお取り替えいたします。